▶

Landing in Las Vegas

WILBUR S. SHEPPERSON SERIES IN NEVADA HISTORY

Landing in Las Vegas ✈

COMMERCIAL AVIATION

AND THE MAKING

OF A TOURIST CITY

Daniel K. Bubb

University of Nevada Press ▲▲ *Reno & Las Vegas*

WILBUR S. SHEPPERSON SERIES IN NEVADA HISTORY
Series Editor: Michael Green

University of Nevada Press, Reno, Nevada 89557 USA
Copyright © 2012 by University of Nevada Press
All rights reserved
Manufactured in the United States of America
Design by Kathleen Szawiola

Library of Congress Cataloging-in-Publication Data

Bubb, Daniel K. (Daniel Kenneth)
Landing in Las Vegas : commercial aviation and the making of a tourist
city / Daniel K. Bubb.
    p. cm. — (Wilbur S. Shepperson series in Nevada history)
Includes bibliographical references and index.
ISBN 978-0-87417-872-2 (cloth : alk. paper) — ISBN 978-0-87417-876-0 (ebook)
1. Aeronautics, Commercial—Nevada—Las Vegas—History. 2. Airlines—
Nevada—Las Vegas—History. 3. Tourism—Nevada—Las Vegas—History.
4. Las Vegas (Nev.)—History. 5. Las Vegas (Nev.)—Economic conditions.
I. Title.
HE9803.A3B83 2012
387.7'4209793135—dc23   2012000651

The paper used in this book is a recycled stock made from 30 percent post-
consumer waste materials, certified by FSC, and meets the requirements
of American National Standard for Information Sciences—Permanence of
Paper for Printed Library Materials, ANSI/NISO Z39.48-1992 (R2002).
Binding materials were selected for strength and durability.

FIRST PRINTING
21   20   19   18   17   16   15   14   13   12
5   4   3   2   1

►

To my parents who have given me so much,

and to my wife, best friend, and the love of my life, Jennifer

Thank You

►

Contents

Illustrations

Acknowledgments

*T*his book is the culmination of ten years of research and writing about the role of commercial aviation in the growth and development of Las Vegas and personal experience as a former airline pilot based in Las Vegas. It is the product of a master's thesis and a doctoral dissertation.

There are several people I would like to thank who helped make this book possible, but because of spatial constraints I will not be able to mention each one of them, for which I apologize. I am deeply grateful to my dissertation director, John Herron, and to Dennis Merrill, Louis Potts, Max Skidmore, and David Atkinson at the University of Missouri, Kansas City, all of whom were instrumental in helping me shape and constantly improve this study through their meticulous reading and insightful suggestions. Other mentors to whom I am indebted for providing helpful comments are Eugene Moehring, Hal Rothman, and David Wrobel at the University of Nevada, Las Vegas.

I would like to thank Dennis McBride and his staff at the Nevada State Historical Museum for their helpfulness in tracking down early photographs of commercial aviation. Similarly, I would like to thank Mark Hall Patton and his staff at the Howard Cannon Aviation Museum in Las Vegas for finding and allowing me to include modern images of airliners and of McCarran Airport. Many thanks go to Matt Becker, acquisitions editor of the University of Nevada Press, for his instrumental guidance and patience throughout the book-publishing process. Marie Force of Delta Airlines was very helpful, sending me primary sources on Western Air Express from the Delta Airlines Archival Center. I also would like to thank Clark County directors of aviation Randall Walker and Bob Broadbent, and John Hanks, manager of international marketing for McCarran Airport, for their generosity in allowing me to interview them. My sincere thanks go to TWA executive station manager Duane Busch, Southwest Airlines marketing representative Susan Davis, America West Airlines marketing manager Jennifer Myers, Beehive

Press executive Richard Taylor (former general manager of the Hacienda Hotel), former Hacienda Airlines chief pilot Boyd Michael, and Rio Resort and Casino director of hotel operations Wanda Chan for the time they spent with me. I would like to thank Michael Maher of the Nevada Historical Society and Peter Michele of the University of Nevada, Las Vegas, for granting me access to primary source materials from the collections of Nevada senators Patrick McCarran, Alan Bible, and Howard Cannon.

I would like to thank my colleagues Michael Green, Sondra Cosgrove, Shirley Johnston, Claytee White, Melise Leech, and Sue Kim Chung at the University of Nevada, Las Vegas, and the College of Southern Nevada for their continuous support and encouragement throughout this endeavor. Also, special thanks go to my colleagues at Missouri Valley College, William Woods University, and Gonzaga University for their endless encouragement. I also am deeply indebted to my students from the College of Southern Nevada, William Woods University, Missouri Valley College, and Gonzaga University, who taught me much about life and humility, and inspired me to continue striving to be the best teacher and mentor I can be.

Finally, I thank my parents, Ken and Donna, my brother, Ken, and my wife, Jennifer, for their support, love, and patience. Without them, this work would not have been possible.

Landing in Las Vegas

▶

Introduction

The airlines of America are the vital core of the world's biggest
industry—travel and tourism.   THOMAS PETZINGER JR.

*T*he typical evening rush hour at McCarran International Airport in Las
Vegas, Nevada, is quite a sight. Air traffic controllers sequence Delta,
Alaska, Southwest, American, Frontier, United, Virgin Atlantic, Northwest,
and Allegiant airliners to land on Runways 25L and 19R. More than two
dozen other passenger jets wait to take off on Runways 25R and 19L. During
the wait, the line of lights in the distance gets longer as more of the world's
finest airliners are sequenced to land at the nation's seventh-busiest and
sixth-largest mega-port.

Manned flight has intrigued Americans from the day the Wright brothers
successfully flew their experimental powered glider *Kitty Hawk* in North Caro-
lina, on December 17, 1903, right up to the landing of the six-hundred-passen-
ger Emirates Airbus A3XX jumbo jet at John F. Kennedy International Airport
on August 1, 2008. Numerous books, articles, and stories have been written
about the phenomenon of man leaving the ground to enter a new frontier in
the sky through passenger travel. Few of them, however, have addressed the
history of what happened when the sky frontier met the ground frontier in
the American East and rapidly moved to the American West.

As the airplane came west to Denver, San Francisco, Los Angeles, Salt Lake
City, Phoenix, and Tucson, these growing cities eagerly reached out to the
new transportation phenomenon by building airports with graded runways,
small terminal buildings, and hotels, working diligently to become part of
the prestigious, government-funded, transcontinental air mail and passenger transportation system. As this system began to grow, smaller connecting
towns were needed for fuel stops, one of which was Las Vegas. An interesting
and previously unexamined part of this story is the meeting of the airplane

with this small desert frontier town in the 1920s and the resulting symbiotic relationship that, over the remaining eight decades of the twentieth century, transformed the tiny oasis into a leading global tourist destination. Why an unexamined story? The reason is that commercial air travel often is taken for granted, viewed simply as a faster and more convenient form of transportation, and Las Vegas has been dismissed as an aberration, a bastion of vice and gambling.

As a new and unseasoned form of transportation and part of the Contract Air Mail Route 4 (CAM-4), commercial air travel came to a sparsely populated Las Vegas in 1926, when the town was little more than a watering hole, an isolated train stop in the desert. During the Great Depression years, when only the wealthy could afford to fly, the airlines struggled, while Las Vegas, with the construction of the Hoover Dam, experienced a tourism boom. During the war years, civilian passenger travel was put on hold so the airlines could provide planes and personnel for the war effort. But the postwar boom and the beginning of the consumer age prompted larger and faster planes to bring more tourists to Las Vegas. McCarran Field expanded its runways and terminal, new casino-resorts appeared downtown, and the city grew. During this time, commercial aviation became a more important source of transportation for tourists, business travelers, and conventioneers wanting to come to the Strip's most recent and most luxurious casino-resorts. The coming of jets in the 1960s revolutionized commercial air travel for the next four decades, offering affordability, comfort, and speed to domestic and global travelers. By century's end, the airlines delivered more than 33 million passengers to McCarran International Airport, with the airlines and airport together pumping more than $30 billion into the southern Nevada economy.[1] Las Vegas reached its zenith as the fastest-growing city in the nation, which in partnership with the largest airline industry in the world and a cutting-edge modern mega-port, formed a world-class travel destination.

I argue here that commercial air passenger transportation, prodded by progressive government aeronautical policies and aviation technology from 1926 to 2009, served as a vital catalyst for Las Vegas's development of a lucrative tourism industry and for the city's rapid growth. I examine the complex relationships among airline technology, airline management, tourism, airport management, and the casino-resorts, and I also highlight the relationships among politics, economics, and technology and explores how these forces combined to shape and reshape Las Vegas's urban growth and development.

The Las Vegas story is a microcosm of the broader regional and national story of the influential role played by airlines and government in the economic growth and development of urban tourism. Close historic ties between commercial passenger travel and the economic growth and vitality of Las Vegas within the broader context of aviation history and the history of the American West are everywhere visible in the concurrent growth of the airline industry, McCarran Airport, and the city.

In exploring the complex relationships between private interests, especially in the air transportation industry, and local, state, and federal governments, I draw on the work of scholars who have emphasized the role played by organized corporations and groups within the U.S. liberal capitalist system. Rationality and efficiency do not come about merely through the marketplace or by political fiat. It is the influence of business groups, labor unions, and other interests together with government action that have made modern capitalism functional. This was certainly true of the airline industry in the United States. Historian Ellis Hawley observed the importance of government involvement in the aviation industry, claiming, "Rapid development of the [aviation] industry was vital to national defense; yet because it was in a pioneer stage, risky, speculative, and unable to offer assured returns, the industry on its own could never attempt the large capital outlays that were necessary for rapid expansion. The answer was government support. Under aviation acts of 1925 and 1926, the government had to step in to provide safety controls, generous mail subsidies, and a wide variety of promotional and navigation aids."[2] These new regulations made air travel much safer and more accessible to the public. Among the cities that would benefit from the federal regulations was Las Vegas.

The resort city made an ideal case study because it is an example of federal, state, and local governments and private entities working together to create unique partnerships that enabled a modern twentieth-century city to rise from the desert floor and become a global tourist mecca. As a once small desert town with a limited economy, Las Vegas financially benefited from private Southern California investment, government funding for an airport meeting strict regulatory standards, revenue from a mushrooming tourism industry, and eventually, an image transformation into a modern metropolis designed to attract domestic and international air travelers. By the twenty-first century, Las Vegas had truly become a world-class travel destination.

CHAPTER ONE

The Airlines Come to Las Vegas

*A*pril 17, 1926, was a landmark day for the dusty little desert town of Las Vegas. At 10:05 A.M., after a two-hour, twenty-nine-minute flight from Los Angeles, Western Air Express World War I pilot Maury Graham landed his single-engine Douglas M-2 biplane on the freshly graded dirt airstrip at the new, officially designated Rockwell Field. Having completed the first leg of the inaugural airmail flight from Los Angeles to Salt Lake City, he stopped in Las Vegas just long enough to refuel and deliver and pick up mailbags, then took off to complete the last leg of his trip. Three hours later, fellow Western Air Express pilot Jimmie James landed at Rockwell Field after a bumpy five-hour, forty-minute flight from Salt Lake City.[1] As planned, he also stopped to refuel and deliver and pick up mailbags, and then continued on to Los Angeles to finish the history-making eight-hour trip. Scheduled commercial aviation had finally come to Las Vegas.

Mayor Fred Hess and excited townspeople turned out to greet both of the pilots as their M-2s arrived. Since 1918, Las Vegans had watched World War I pilots Randall Henderson and Emery Rogers arrive from Southern California in their small Curtiss JN-4 "Jennies" doing flybys and touch-and-gos to impress their desert onlookers with the wonders of this new machine called the aeroplane. Henderson, Rogers, and other pilots "just dropped in as if it were an everyday occurrence to hop across 300 miles of desert to call on friends."[2]

Of course, an essential part of the promotion of aviation in Las Vegas was landing and parking the planes for public inspection, as well as offering flights to the daring, of which there always were a few. Most Las Vegans were left with "dislocated necks and sunburned tonsils" from watching the planes circle the valley. Army Air Corps pilots also frequently performed aerial maneuvers over the little town in their De Havilland DH-4s while scouting airmail routes. Being able to get a firsthand look at the M-2 biplanes, with their mailbag compartments in the front and pilot seating in the back, was a big deal on this special occasion. Robert Griffith, then the postmaster of Las Vegas, recalled "the great day of April 17, 1926 when Jimmie James landed at Las Vegas. . . . Several hundred people watched as 'Wild Bill' Morgan, former Pony Express rider, delivered the first bag of mail on horseback ever to be sent from Las Vegas by air. . . . Jimmie was a well loved hero and the plane was the finest. The Douglas M-2 had a 450 hp engine, metal prop, droppable gas tanks, 145 mile per hour speed, many other up to the minute features, and cost a fabulous $18,000 dollars. . . . Las Vegas, for sure was on the map now."[3]

This level of excitement for a pair of airmail pilots delivering a few bags of letters may seem overblown (671 letters to Las Vegas and 2,246 letters to Los Angeles and Salt Lake City), but Postmaster Griffith was correct: Las Vegas was literally on the national aviation map now. As a fuel stop on the Los Angeles–to–Salt Lake City feeder route, Las Vegas became a part of the highly coveted San Francisco–to–New York transcontinental airmail system, which opened the door to passenger travel and tourism. And with the guidance and financial support of the federal government, during the next eight decades commercial airlines enabled Las Vegas to become a world-class travel and tourism destination.

Using aviation to transform Las Vegas was a massive undertaking, but it started simply enough, with the airmail. At the end of World War I, many Americans wondered about the complex shift from combat to peace. Questions about the shape of the American economy, the role of the federal government in private life, and the place of the military in a peacetime society headlined contemporary debates. Several of these concerns telescoped into the issue of aviation.

Near the conclusion of World War I, the federal government began experimenting with transporting mail by air because of the speed of delivery. Army Air Corps pilots were the best trained and the most experienced at flying, and after the war there was an abundance of them. So the U.S. Post Office hired them to transport the mail. On May 15, 1918, President Woodrow Wilson ordered the allocation of $100,000 for pilots, airplanes, maintenance personnel, and facilities for the U.S. Post Office to transport part of the nation's mail by air from New York to Washington, D.C., via Philadelphia. To save money, the Post Office purchased the cheapest and most available of the World War I surplus planes, the JN-4 "Jennies," but found that their airframes were too fragile and their engines failed during flight. The Post Office then changed to the larger De Havilland DH-4, which could carry 400 pounds of mail and travel 250 miles before refueling, but that plane proved not to be fuel-efficient for long-distance flight. Needing more durable planes, the Post Office switched to the workhorse Douglas M-2, which could carry more than 1,000 pounds of mail, could travel 600 miles without refueling, and had a more reliable engine.

For the airmail industry to be successful, flight safety was paramount. Even with better planes and highly skilled pilots, the Army Air Corps from 1918 to 1927 had more than two hundred crashes, causing forty-three deaths and twenty-five serious injuries. The reasons for the crashes were many. With an increasingly heavy business mail volume demanding time-saving delivery, there was immense pressure for round-the-clock mail service. To meet deadlines, pilots had to fly day and night, often in adverse weather conditions. Airplane cockpits lacked proper navigation instruments, forcing pilots to practice "iron navigation," pilot jargon for following the railroad tracks, and keeping to the right. Night flying was especially precarious because in most places there was no safe ground lighting. Pioneer pilots literally had to "fly by the seat of their pants," a reality that caused the most daring among them to be chosen to fly the mail routes. A crash report from well-known pioneer mail pilot Dean Smith is informative: "On Trip 4 westbound. Flying low. Engine quit. Only place to land on cow. Killed cow. Wrecked plane. Scared me. Smith."[4]

By 1924 marginal improvement was made in flight safety when the Army Air Corps installed turn indicators in airplane cockpits, gyroscopic instruments that enabled pilots to see when and how much they were turning in low-visibility flying conditions. That same year, the federal government began installing flashing beacons on hilltops, and by 1927, airmail pilots could fly 4,121 miles of lit airways nationwide at night, visibility depending on weather conditions. Though these changes provided some measure of safety, pioneer airmail flying was still dangerous.

The 1920s mail planes were built of light wood and fabric, often incapable of handling turbulent flying conditions. Many a wing or tail blew off in strong winds and storms. Lightning caused fires, and flocks of birds damaged engines. With weak regulatory oversight, airplane maintenance was poor. An added problem was that the now-underfunded Army Air Corps tried to save money by delaying airplane overhauls as long as possible.

All of these difficulties hampered the effort to create a viable airmail delivery infrastructure, thus giving the airmail division of the Post Office a bad reputation among the public as both unreliable and unsafe. Additionally, railroad executives complained to Congress that the Post Office's airmail division was cutting into their profits. They approached Representative M. Clyde Kelly (R-Pa.), a strong supporter of the railroads, asking him to persuade his congressional colleagues to privatize airmail transportation to force the Post Office's aviation division out of business. The railroads could then try to control the airlines through majority stock ownership. With mounting pressure from railroad executives, and the public's concern about lack of aviation safety, in 1924 Postmaster General Harry New terminated the Post Office's contract with the Army Air Corps.

The Army Air Corps departure paved the way for powerful private commercial airline businessmen such as Juan Trippe, a Yale University graduate, cofounder of New York Airways, and later CEO of Pan American Airways (Pan Am), and Harris M. "Pop" Hanshue, a former Southern California race car driver and automobile dealership owner who was president of Western Air Express Airlines, to use their influence to further pressure Congress to privatize airmail transportation. Trippe especially pushed for privatization so he could build a globally competitive commercial airline mail and passenger service from the East Coast of the United States to Central and South America. At the same time, both men recognized that even if Congress approved privatization, the airline industry still would need some government financial backing because private financial funding alone was insufficient. With the help of Alan Scaife, a fellow Yale graduate and a son of the prominent Scaife family, which owned several ore mining businesses in Pittsburgh, Trippe petitioned Representative Kelly to craft legislation allowing private companies to contract with the Post Office to transport the mail.[5]

Embracing his party's free-market, laissez-faire political ideology, Kelly responded by presenting to Congress a proposal that authorized the postmaster general to contract with private carriers, set airmail rates, and decide how much to subsidize the airlines. On February 2, 1925, Congress passed the Kelly Act. Immediately, more than twenty private air carriers placed bids for contracts with the Post Office, including Las Vegas's first airline, Western Air Express.

As far back as October 1920, there was talk in southern Nevada of a possible airmail route passing through Las Vegas. An editorial in the *Clark County Review* pointed out how the original postal air route from San Francisco to Salt Lake City via Reno was too dangerous because of the Sierra Nevada's high elevation, blinding winter blizzards, and severe up- and downdrafts during the hot summer. The editorial claimed that Las Vegas, located away from the mountains in the flat Mojave Desert, would be a much safer and more suitable stopping point for aircraft to refuel.[6] Robert Hausler, a Las Vegan and former army pilot scouting airmail routes in the Southwest, agreed with the newspaper. So, in November 1920, he prepared tiny Anderson Field with a leveled L-shaped runway for takeoffs and landings and built a small terminal and a fuel station.

The newspaper praised Hausler, stating, "With the establishing of Anderson Field, which is due principally to the efforts of Bob Hausler, and the reputed price of these machines [airplanes], which is not more than a good auto, it is not unreasonable to suppose that one or more machines will soon be located here for commercial purposes and possibly some privately owned."[7] The new airfield drew praise from the Southern California Aero Club, an organization comprising wealthy businessmen and former World War I pilots interested in promoting and increasing aviation in Southern California.

The club believed that promoting Las Vegas as a fuel stop for eastern travelers heading west would increase air travel in Los Angeles and enable Southern California to compete with Northern California for aviation business (San Francisco was the West Coast terminal on the transcontinental airmail route). Establishing a Post Office airmail route through Las Vegas would assist this endeavor by increasing air traffic and bringing greater publicity to the region through airmail advertising. Hausler and the Aero Club published an article in *Aviation and Aircraft Journal* explaining why the Post Office should select Las Vegas to be part of the Los Angeles–to–Salt Lake City Contract Air Mail Route 4 (CAM-4). They wrote: "Las Vegas has the best laid out and properly marked [air]field between Salt Lake and Los Angeles."[8]

To drum up local support for the Contract Air Mail Route 4 bid, the editor of the *Clark County Review* released this statement: "The value of the airmail to Las Vegas cannot be overestimated: aside from the convenience of the service, the inauguration of this new route will bring a vast amount of publicity for this city, which could not be purchased at any price. It is in the interest of every businessman of this city that he avail himself of the new means of communication at every opportunity."[9] No effort seemed too great to attract airmail delivery to the city. The newspaper asked Las Vegans to "write their friends and send them a letter on the first plane out of here, for the continuance of the service will depend on the amount of business done."[10]

Essentially, the Post Office needed "feeder routes" to pick up and deliver mail and promote aviation in smaller towns off the main transcontinental route from San Francisco to New York, one of which was the CAM-4 Los Angeles–to–Salt Lake City route. Feeder routes also provided fuel stops because mail planes often did not have the fuel range to make nonstop flights. In Nevada, pilots repeatedly complained to Postmaster Robert Griffith about not being able to complete their flights because their airplanes kept running out of gas. Clearly, a series of connected stopover cities was required. Although other Nevada towns such as Caliente, Pioche, and Ely also wanted to be on the route, they could not compete with Las Vegas's natural advantages of long, wide valleys for airplanes to safely take off and land. Mayor Fred Hess and Postmaster Robert Griffith tried to convince U.S. Postmaster General Harry S. New that since Las Vegas was farther south than its competitors, it would be a wise choice as a fuel stop for a southern transcontinental airmail route. The country had a northern and a central transcontinental airmail route, but not a southern one. A southern route would facilitate expansion of airmail volume, allow faster delivery to southern towns, and generate more revenue from increased business for the Post Office, private air carriers, and towns being served. After a five-year effort, the newspaper editorials, political support, and pressure from the Southern California Aero Club finally succeeded: on November 7, 1925, Griffith announced that Las Vegas would be an official stopping point on the CAM-4 Route.[11]

Soon after Griffith made the announcement, the news made headlines in the *Clark County Review,* and the entire town went crazy with excitement. The city council rejoiced and was overwhelmed by the deluge of positive responses from the public in the form of phone calls and letters. The newspaper proclaimed: "Over one hundred letters have already been received at the post office to be mailed out on the first mail plane leaving here, some of them being sent long distances."[12] Las Vegans eagerly awaited the arrival of a commercial plane to transport their letters, but a public accustomed to the rickety planes of the Army Air Corps never imagined that plane would be as impressive as the Douglas M-2, part of Harris M. "Pop" Hanshue's Western Air Express fleet.

Hanshue, along with William Garland, a wealthy Realtor, Harry Chandler, owner and publisher of the *Los Angeles Times,* and James A. Talbot of Richfield Oil, saw a lucrative opportunity offered by the federal government to start a feeder airline service to the central transcontinental airmail route. With Chandler, Garland, and Talbot as primary financiers and Hanshue as president, they started a feeder airline company called Western Air Express, based in Glendale. Its initial public offering was 4,283 shares of stock valued at $100 per share.[13] The revenue from the stock was used to purchase flying equipment, build hangars, and construct terminal facilities. Western Air Express's fleet consisted of six Douglas M-2s and three Fokker 10s, all of which were used to fly mail from Los Angeles to Salt Lake City with a stop in Las Vegas, Cheyenne to Pueblo, Amarillo to Dallas, and Los Angeles to Kansas City. The airline made a profit of $1,140 per flight hauling mail, which was considerable for that time, but slowly diminished as insurance and operating costs later increased.[14] Originally, the interest of Western Air Express was hauling mail, but Hanshue had a different goal—he wanted to transport people.

In 1926 his opportunity came with a grant for $180,000 from the Guggenheim Fund for the Advancement of Aeronautics to establish a route between San Francisco and Los Angeles. Using three Fokker 10s with seating for twelve passengers, the new business began slowly, with the transportation of six hundred passengers that year.[15] Two years later, more than five thousand passengers had traveled the route, confirming Hanshue's vision that there was growing demand for airplanes to haul mail and people. In a reminiscence, W. W. Hawes, second assistant postmaster general in Washington, D.C., recalled how, "although no mail contract was obtained for this route, and Western Air Express's operation [initially] resulted in considerable loss, nevertheless the Los Angeles to San Francisco route was warranted by the development of additional air transportation service which gained for Western Air Express an unexcelled reputation for service, and which further provided experience and data necessary for the future expansion of passenger and air mail operations." With financial support from the government, the commercial air travel industry could not fail. As Hawes noted, "The Post Office Department, in its role of sponsor of commercial air transportation development, established the policy of desiring and aiding the expansion of efficient, safe, and economical air passenger transportation."[16] Though the airlines got their start by transporting mail, Trippe, Hanshue, and other airline executives always had the broader vision of transporting people.

Although the intent of the Kelly Act was to allow private air carriers to transport mail, it soon gave way to the Air Commerce Act of 1926, which permitted air carriers to transport passengers. While the Post Office had been building the airmail system, the government had begun experimenting immediately after World War I with the idea of expanding aviation to carry people. Government officials did not have to look far. Most European states had already begun passenger air travel. This was not the first time the United States fell behind Europe in air travel and aviation technology. According to aviation historian Roger Bilstein, "As early as 1911, many thoughtful figures in American aviation circles believed that the United States had begun to fall behind in comparison to European aeronautics. France, Russia, Germany, Italy, and Great Britain all had active aeronautical laboratories with varying degrees of government support, and many of their designs were beginning to show clear evidence of superiority over American aircraft."[17] A scathing report by Dr. Albert F. Zahm, chief of the Smithsonian Aviation Laboratory, confirmed this, according to Bilstein, who wrote that the 1914 report "emphasized the galling disparity between European progress and American inertia."[18] This disparity meant that Europe became the leader in aviation technology and had the ability to dominate global markets. The Air Commerce Act sought to improve commercial aviation by creating a regulatory aviation framework to better organize it, make air travel safer, establish an agency to supervise it, and enable the U.S. commercial aviation industry to compete globally with the European air carriers. But which U.S. government agency would oversee the airlines?

The logical agency to address the need seemed to be the Department of Commerce. While the Republican administrations of the 1920s are popularly associated with free-market economics, numerous historians have shown that the government structures established during the Progressive Era endured through the Roaring Twenties and in some cases underwent expansion. The historian Joan Hoff Wilson has in fact identified Secretary of Commerce Herbert Hoover as a "forgotten progressive" who used his regulatory powers to streamline domestic commerce and greatly expand U.S. foreign trade.[19] He used the same approach to reorganize the airline industry.

Hoover understood aviation's economic value to the United States, and his newly established Bureau of Aeronautics in the Department of Commerce established a basic and badly needed aviation regulatory framework. Its laws were based on the secretary's seven-pronged vision: creating a system of national airways, subsidizing private companies to transport the mail, making the commercial aviation industry an auxiliary to national defense, regulating pilots and planes to increase safety, getting government completely out of transporting mail by plane, allocating funding for scientific research into aviation problems, and creating a separate governmental agency to supervise the aviation industry. Hoover's plan resulted from the findings of a panel of representatives of airplane manufacturing companies, aeronautical engineers, and public officials who urged the establishment of a strong regulatory system for planes and pilots that could reverse the existing pattern of too many crashes from poorly constructed and maintained planes, and insufficiently experienced pilots.[20]

Hoover was not the only government official who could imagine a profitable commercial aviation industry operating within a strong governmental regulatory framework. President Calvin Coolidge also envisioned the beginning of an industry that would be a major stimulus to national, state, and local economies, while also recognizing the importance of air safety. After the passage of the Kelly Act of 1925, he appointed a task force led by Dwight Morrow, a former college classmate of his, a senior partner at J. P. Morgan, and later a U.S. senator, to investigate the feasibility of safe mail and passenger transportation. The Morrow Report concluded that the airline industry would provide an important service to the nation but needed to be subsidized by the government through mail contracts so that commercial air travel could be made profitable and safe. Similar to Hoover's plan, the Morrow Report recommended government provision for air routes, a weather warning system, airway charts, partial funding for landing fields and airports, lit airways for night flying, systematic inspection of planes and personnel to ensure safe and reliable transportation, and a limit on contract airmail carriage holding it to no more than 80 percent of postal receipts.[21]

Essentially, the Morrow Report recommended that a private airline industry funded by the federal government would create the foundation for what the government and airlines hoped would be a growing, thriving, modern mass transportation industry. The new agency, in keeping with the findings of the Morrow Commission, would mandate that the Department of Commerce certify airplanes for airworthiness, require pilots to pass flight tests and written examinations, and provide funding for adequate navigation aids, including color-coded flashing beacons so planes could fly at night.[22] It would also regulate airfares. On May 20, 1926, President Calvin Coolidge made that happen by signing into law the Air Commerce Act. An equally important provision of the act ensured the preservation of government-private business relations in the aviation industry.

On May 23, 1926, just five weeks after the arrival of the first mail plane and mere days after the passage of the Air Commerce Act, a Western Air Express Douglas M-2 coming from Los Angeles delivered its first passengers, A. B. DeNault, vice president of the Piggly-Wiggly grocery chain, and Charles Kerr, president of the Los Angeles Automobile Insurance Company, to Las

Vegas. That same day, a southbound Western Air Express M-2 arrived from Salt Lake City with passengers Benjamin F. Redman, chairman of the Aviation Committee of the Salt Lake City Chamber of Commerce, and John A. Tomlinson, a businessman from Salt Lake City. Redman and Tomlinson were honorary guests celebrating the inauguration of Western Air Express's first passenger flights from Salt Lake City to Las Vegas.[23] When they deplaned, they were welcomed by Harris M. "Pop" Hanshue, president of Western Air Express, Las Vegas mayor Fred Hess, Las Vegas townspeople, and even a few dogs. They were also greeted by eager local news reporters for the *Clark County Review,* who asked them about their flight experience. Redman and Tomlinson enjoyed the adventure of the five-hour, forty-minute flight, bumps and all, aboard the faithful M-2, a single-engine, open-cockpit biplane flying at a speed of 135 miles per hour and an altitude of 6,000 feet.[24] As they spoke to the news reporters, they removed their primitive flight gear—coveralls, leather helmets, goggles, and parachutes.

The publicity of Redman and Tomlinson's arrival attracted the attention of many others present who wanted to fly on the Western Air Express plane. Hollywood celebrity and nationally recognized aviation supporter Will Rogers, who happened to be shooting part of a film in Las Vegas at the time and never turned down a chance to fly and promote aviation, begged to be the first passenger to fly with Jimmie James on to Los Angeles. With such a large volume of mail that day, there was no room for a passenger, so James politely refused. Rogers offered to buy as many postage stamps as necessary to pay for his weight, but he never got his ride.

Maude Campbell, a telephone supervisor and public relations clerk from Salt Lake City, became the first female passenger to fly to Los Angeles on Western Air Express. Wanting to enjoy the warm weather in Southern California, Campbell paid $90 to fly round-trip from Salt Lake City to Los Angeles on June 10, 1926, with an overnight stop in Las Vegas. The flight took six hours and fifty minutes each way in the M-2. Campbell, who donned a flight suit, golf knickers, and a parachute, sat on mailbags for the entire flight. If anything catastrophic happened to the plane en route, she was told, she should jump, count to three, and pull the cord.[25] Upon her arrival in Los Angeles, Campbell was greeted by photographers, journalists, and "Pop" Hanshue, who gave her a bouquet of flowers. Campbell made national news and her picture appeared on the front page of the *New York Times* as the first female in the United States to travel on an airline. She expressed her excitement about flying, but found the seat uncomfortable and the engine noisy.

The arrival of DeNault, Kerr, Redman, Tomlinson, Campbell, and later other customers interested in the many business and leisure possibilities of air travel signified to the Las Vegas community that the airline industry had great potential in their city as an important transportation source for a future business and desert tourist industry. Undoubtedly some travelers would only pass through Las Vegas and, like the planes they traveled in, replenish themselves, then move on. But as R. W. Martin, S. R. Whitehead, S. J. Lawson, A. S. Henderson, and other members of the board of directors of the Las Vegas Chamber of Commerce correctly predicted, many others would come and want to stay.[26] Those passengers who stayed would eventually transform the economic livelihood of the city. City officials and commercial airline promoters began to build a plan for Las Vegas as a resort destination vitally linked to commercial passenger aviation. While these events might seem like a series of publicity stunts advertising a new mode of transportation that was unaffordable for most people, the Las Vegas Chamber of Commerce regarded them as business opportunities for the future development of Las Vegas as a tourist city.

Tom Grimshaw, a Los Angeles newspaper reporter, foresaw aviation's bright future in Las Vegas and the West after his first ride in an M-2 with Western Air Express pioneer mail pilot Al DiGarmo in September of that year. He wrote, "The Pony Express and the hero riders who carried the mail for the West are far in the dim past. The stagecoach and its swash-buckling drivers are only a memory in the minds of the oldest, but today their successors, as daring a crew as ever gathered, are hurtling through the air with their cargoes of mail [and passengers] sailing high over mountains, deserts, and buffeting storms. . . . They are pioneers in their field, blazing the way for what will tomorrow be a great air transportation system of the West."[27] Western Air Express was ready to transport more travelers to Las Vegas, but was Anderson Field adequate?

Before Las Vegas was chosen for the CAM-4 route, the townspeople were happy to have Anderson Field with its general aviation activity, but Mayor Fred Hess and airport manager Robert Hausler became concerned about its insufficient runway length and lack of proper facilities for larger airmail and passenger planes. A letter from the Southern California Aero Club to the *Clark County Review* predicted that "there would be a very rapid advance in aerial transportation. Communities may need large air terminals or be passed up entirely because they are not prepared. This is just as important to Las Vegas as [it is] to Los Angeles or San Francisco, for [commercial] aviation will bring Nevada and Arizona towns as close to other commercial centers as the railroad now connects New York and Washington or Philadelphia."[28] Even Colonel Swen Laetsew of the Southwest Region of the Post Office had warned Hausler of the need for a more appropriate airfield if Las Vegas were to be chosen for Contract Air Mail Route-4. He asserted it would be up to Las Vegas to "prepare the airplane mail route by having a landing field and by building a hangar. It is impossible to consider any city as a landing place that does not offer adequate facilities."[29] Both funds and a new field were needed.

Like other small Nevada towns such as Ely, Elko, and Reno, Las Vegas could not rely on the federal and state governments to provide much funding for airport expansion because larger, already established commercial airports like San Francisco, Los Angeles, and Seattle received the bulk of the available funding. Since many of these cities' airports were hubs (the primary base) for the airlines, and the busiest in terms of air traffic and passenger volume, they received most of any federal moneys. The federal government believed that cities should provide the bulk of the funding for airport construction and expansion. Historians Ellis Armstrong, Michael Robinson, and Suellen Hoy have written that "the 1926 Air Commerce Act had authorized the Secretary of Commerce to establish, operate, and maintain civil airways, but left the airports to be provided for on a local basis. Until the mid 1930s, airport development remained, for the most part, the responsibility of private investors and local government units."[30] Las Vegas had another challenge as well: finding adequate land upon which to build newer and better airports. This became a thorny issue, especially with the Bureau of Land Management, which was known for its parsimony in land distribution and development in southern Nevada. Essentially, local airports had to find and rely on private funding, and Las Vegas was no exception.

In early April 1926, the city approached Leon and Earl Rockwell, two local businessmen and landowners. The brothers initially were reluctant to lease their property to the city because they believed building an airport on it would decrease its value. This situation not only would have left the city in a tenuous situation, but it would have left Harris Hanshue, president of Western Air Express, without an airport. It also directly threatened the Contract Air Mail Route 4 deal with the Post Office. Newspaper headlines dramatized the volatile situation. One article stated that "not having an airport was among the most pressing problems the City Council faced."[31] Without airmail, Las Vegans would have had to depend on the old Post Office mail delivery system by train, which took much longer than delivery by plane. More significantly, the absence of airmail would mean losing out on becoming an important participant in this new and exciting mode of transportation. Postmaster Griffith, Hausler, and the Las Vegas Chamber of Commerce persuaded the Rockwell brothers that their property would not decline in value but in fact would increase because the city would pay them above-market rates for their land and would charge Western Air Express fees for takeoff and landing to cover airport expenses. Western Air Express was guaranteed an airport.

The Chamber of Commerce immediately set up a committee to raise funds to clear and properly equip the field, and offered Hanshue rent-free use of the field for one year. Years later, Postmaster Griffith reminisced how "Leon and Earl Rockwell were very generous to let us use some of their land. The property had been the site of a former 'road house' which had failed and burned to the ground, but the operator had built a power line and dug a well. These proved to be most valuable assets—the beacon light was a Westinghouse and had a windmill tower. The County provided a tractor and the Union Pacific Railroad Company 'lent' a length of steel rail which was pulled over the surface to knock down the sagebrush and fill small holes. A radio shack, ten by twelve, wood siding, and a pump and small tank were furnished by Western Air Express and we were in business."[32] Chamber of Commerce president R. W. Martin and board of directors members K. O. Knudson, L. J. Oakes, O. A. Kimball, and W. J. Hooper sent a letter to the county and city commissioners urging them to purchase the land from the Rockwell brothers. They did, and in 1927 Las Vegas had its airline and airport. But was the city ready to be a destination?

Las Vegas, meaning "the meadows," historically was green with grasses, willows, and cottonwoods growing from its many aquifers. Located in a southwestern Nevada desert valley surrounded by mountains and hills, in the nineteenth century it served as an oasis for the Paiute Indians, early Spanish explorers, fur trappers, mountain men, and frontiersmen. Wagon trains followed the well-used cutoff from the Old Spanish Trail through the southwest desert to replenish their stores of water from Las Vegas Creek before continuing to California.

Because of its abundance of water, in 1901 U.S. senator William A. Clark, a wealthy copper king from Montana and a western railroad baron, saw to it that the last link of the Union Pacific Transcontinental Railroad from Salt Lake City to Los Angeles passed through Las Vegas. Hundreds of men from all parts of the country came to build Clark's railroad and his desert town, a passenger and freight train center, and a railhead for nearby mines. The town's population consisted of rugged, hardworking railroad men and miners who made sure they had saloons well stocked with free-flowing liquor, gambling, and brothels. Some newcomers built a fancy hotel or two, and the railroad built California bungalow-style cottages for its workers and a large depot, which functioned as the center of the town's economic and social life. In June 1911, with a population of 1,500, Las Vegas was incorporated as a city with full electrical and telephone service.

When the United States entered World War I, the town became a busy depot for the transport of much-needed metals for defense use. But after the war, when the need for ores declined, many businesses went bankrupt. Traveling motorists venturing west, needing supplies and water, stopped in Las Vegas for a short time before continuing to California or other destinations. Some travelers stayed overnight in the town's few small hotels and patronized its local downtown businesses, which Las Vegas historian Eugene Moehring described as a "handful of dry goods stores, cafes, dance halls, saloons, and sawdust-floored casinos."[33] Historian Hal Rothman characterized Las Vegas at the time as "a simple western [railroad] town. The railroad provided a capital regime; it was the only consistent source of funding for the town, and its goals determined those of the city."[34] But the town's goals were not always consistent with those of the railroad.

In 1922 Las Vegas suffered a severe economic crisis when the railroad workers joined the national railroad strike against reduced wages. Vengeful Union Pacific executives moved the company's repair yard, by then the economic life of the city, thirty miles north to Caliente, taking three hundred jobs with them. When the strike ended, Union Pacific closed the Las Vegas repair shops. The economy suffered another blow when the output of gold, silver, copper, rhyolite, and magnesium ores diminished and mining slowing. Hundreds of the town's residents left to find work elsewhere. With just 2,300 residents and no solid economic base, the town seemed to have a bleak future. And yet very unexpectedly, all that was about to change.

With California agriculture pushing for water use of the Colorado River, seven western states, including Nevada, signed the Colorado River Compact in the fall of 1922, agreeing to divide the water equally. But the federal government had bigger plans. It wanted to dam the Colorado River for better irrigation, to provide better water supplies for southwestern cities like San Diego, Las Vegas, and Phoenix, and to produce hydroelectricity for the region. Las Vegas's Black Canyon was chosen as the place to dam the river because of its easy accessibility for the movement of supplies by rail. Six years later, the Boulder Canyon Project Act, the first of a series of bills calling for the construction of a high dam and canal, passed in the U.S. House and Senate. Las Vegans were ecstatic when they learned that the government was going to build the biggest dam in the world in their backyard, and they celebrated in wild Las Vegas style, with the whole town turning out in full force to parade. Despite Prohibition, bootleg liquor flowed like water.

With the federal government appropriating $165 million for the entire project, Las Vegas stood to benefit financially from dam construction as more than $23 million was pumped into the city's economy. Construction required the labor of 5,000 workers, and they brought their families with them to southern Nevada, many moving to Las Vegas, which was only thirty miles away from the dam site.[35] The city assumed that its town would be the permanent headquarters for the project, but its lawless reputation had gotten back to D.C.

When Herbert Hoover, elected president in 1928, sent his secretary of the interior, Wilbur Lyman, to scout out nearby services for workers at the dam site, the city fathers ordered all saloons, gambling clubs, and brothels closed for the visit. Las Vegans put on their best behavior to impress Secretary Lyman with a peaceful tour of their town and respectful observance of the Eighteenth Amendment. It might have worked if local newspaper reporters hadn't invited a friendly member of the secretary's entourage to the wild Arizona Club for a few drinks. The visitor's words of praise to his superiors for such a hospitable town were overshadowed by the strong odor of alcohol on his breath. Las Vegas, it was decided, was too far from the dam site for a commute that could waste precious building time.

A tent city, later called Boulder City, would be constructed near the dam site for the workers and their families, all of whom would be allowed to visit Las Vegas and spend their money there on condition that they didn't imbibe its liquor. The Las Vegas economy got a boost from workers buying food and other necessities as well as patronizing the saloons and brothels, and an even greater boost from tourists arriving from different parts of the country eager to see the Hoover Dam.

When construction of the dam began in 1931, it drew nearly 100,000 tourists from all over the West, the majority of whom arrived by automobile and contributed to the Las Vegas economy with the purchase of goods, gambling, and hospitality in the downtown motels. Three years later, the number of tourists had increased to more than 300,000, from different parts of the world.[36] Las Vegas's economy was booming, but the prosperity was short-lived. In 1935, dam construction ended, and most of the workers and their families left the area to find new jobs. Tourism declined and the Las Vegas economy became weak. It was clearly time for the city to reinvent itself. The casino-resorts had had such a lucrative tourist experience with the building of the dam that city officials and businesspeople realized the city should capitalize on tourism as a substantial source of future revenue. Thus they collaborated on finding ways to promote tourism and recapture much-needed revenues.

They staged golf tournaments, boat races on Lake Mead, rodeos, and parades, marketing the city as a vacation spot in the Old West, but these events interested only a few visitors. The single attraction that brought in the most tourists and the most revenue was gambling. Most of the workers and tourists during the Hoover Dam construction years came to Las Vegas bars and hotel/casinos to gamble. Because Nevada was one of the poorest states in the country, hit hard by both the Great Depression and a steady depletion of its ores, it needed a unique industry that would steadily attract tourists for revenue enhancement.

Legalized gambling finally provided the answer. Gambling had been part of Las Vegas since 1911, and by the early 1930s it enjoyed the support of powerful regional interests. In the 1920s and 1930s, Los Angeles, with its successful movie industry and ever-growing influx of residents, emerged as the western center of entertainment and underground and offshore gambling. The city boasted some of the finest nightclubs and hotels in the country, with international cuisines and first-class services. Gambling was lucrative and widespread, though never legalized. Property owners and operators Tony Cornero, Guy McAfee, and John Grayson attracted enormous crowds of visitors to Los Angeles by building extravagant offshore casinos with luxurious carpeting, chandeliers, fine-dining restaurants, and top entertainment. When the state cracked down on gambling in Los Angeles, Cornero, McAfee, and Grayson set their sights on Las Vegas, where they could build their lavish casinos and offer legal gambling. They sent representatives Johnny Roselli, Murray Humphreys, and Frank Detra to spread mob money throughout the state to persuade legislators to legalize the lucrative vice. Irv Owen, an attorney from Oklahoma and a lifelong friend of Murray Humphreys, remembered: "In the 1930s, Humphreys and his protégé Johnny Roselli bribed the Nevada legislature into legalizing gambling." Journalist Gus Russo wrote: "During the 1930 debate over gambling legalization, young John [son of

Frank Detra] began accompanying his father as he made deliveries of cash-stuffed briefcases and envelopes to influential Nevadans across the state. Frank Detra admitted to his son that the money was being spent to ensure the passage of the Wide-Open Gambling Bill."[37]

But legislators and the governor wanted tighter government regulation of gambling. Assemblyman Phil Tobin stated: "I was just plumb sick and tired of seeing gambling going on all over the state and payoffs being made everywhere. Some of these tinhorn cops were collecting 50 bucks a month for allowing it. Also, the damn state was broke and we needed the money."[38] An editorialist for the *Reese River Reveille* wrote: "If we are going to have gambling . . . let's have it in the open and be honest with ourselves. Regulate the thing and use the revenue for some good purpose."[39] On March 19, 1931, the Nevada Legislature passed the Gaming Act, which contained a provision mandating all counties to regulate gaming, collect fees, and give the state its share. But regulated gaming did not stop the mob from expanding its presence and wealth through the construction of Bel Air–like luxurious resorts and casinos in southern Nevada.

After seeing the small, dated, sawdust-floored casinos in Las Vegas, Cornero, McAfee, Grayson, and others built newer, swankier casinos—the $300,000 Meadows Club, the Pair-O-Dice, and the Pioneer Club. These properties had swamp coolers (an early form of air-conditioning, which made the desert heat more bearable), carpeting, new gaming tables, slot machines, restaurants, and live music, all of which drew large crowds of gamblers from California, northern Nevada, and Arizona.

This new generation of casinos was a major improvement over the old ones, but driving to them was time-consuming, taking hours, even days. Additionally, driving on unpaved highways was uncomfortable. Even after road workers graded, widened, and oiled Highway 91, which connected Los Angeles with Las Vegas, the ruts and bumps still drew complaints from motorists, especially because automobiles of that time lacked shock absorbers. Also, automobiles had no air-conditioning and their engines easily overheated, which made driving through triple-digit desert temperatures dangerous and physically unbearable. There were no roadside services and few repair stations along the route. Nevada historian Elizabeth Harrington notes: "To go by automobile was almost prohibitive, since to travel from Las Vegas to Los Angeles by this means one had to drive by way of Searchlight and Needles with a complete absence of paving of any kind after leaving Las

Vegas until reaching the El Cajon Pass. The trip over this rough road took at least two days and one night of travel. The automobile had much to be desired as far as riding comfort goes."[40] The combination of frustrated motorists and an isolated desert city desperately needing visitors for revenue underscored an urgent need for a better source of mass public transportation, and all answers pointed to the passenger plane.

While Las Vegas is associated in popular culture with legalized gambling, showgirls, and booze, none of those attractions themselves made the western city boom. In the end, it was convenient, affordable air transportation, privately owned and federally funded, that catapulted Las Vegas to nationwide fame. Commercial airplanes traveled more than twice the speed of trains and three times the speed of automobiles. They in essence collapsed geographical distance between isolated Las Vegas and its western counterparts Los Angeles, Phoenix, Salt Lake City, and Denver. In 1926 Western Air Express transported 209 passengers nationwide. In 1928 the tally rose to 6,000, and by 1936 more than 20,000 passengers had flown on the airline.[41]

Commercial air travel was becoming increasingly popular, but it was expensive and quite uncomfortable. Because Ford Tri-Motors, Douglas M-2s, and Fokker 10s were non-pressurized, noisy, and lacked cabin heat, passengers often experienced airsickness, especially in turbulent conditions. And such conditions frequently occurred on hot, windy days, with some flights briefly delayed because ground crews had to hose out the cabins and restock them with barf bags. The airplane was still the fastest mode of transportation, however, significantly reducing travel time and offering a new and exciting experience.

Air travel proved so popular that airline reservations were typically booked up for three to four weeks. On a United Airlines flight from Chicago to San Francisco, with several intermediate stops, including Iowa City, Jane Eads, of the *Chicago Herald and Examiner,* wrote: "Before landing in Iowa City, I was too frightened to write. The plane tipped, tilted, and dropped. I just threw down my pencil and hung on. . . . It was the most exhilarating feeling I've ever experienced in all my life."[42] Marcia Davenport, a writer for the *New Yorker,* wrote this description of her flying experience from Los Angeles to New York with an unscheduled stop at an airfield near Cheyenne, Wyoming: "An automobile trip held to the conveniences of the moment by red-and-white filling stations and hard white roads edged by tourist camps, would not have brought [me] this adventure. It is possible. You can have adventure."[43] The airline industry experienced continued steady growth (more than 173,000 passengers took to the skies in 1929), but that growth did not come without growing pains.[44]

As the Great Depression gripped the United States, many planes flew with empty seats and airlines tried to survive by carrying mail. Some air carriers managed to prevail, though a majority did not. In 1930, forty-four airlines provided service in the country, but by 1933, only five (including mergers) remained in business. One of the survivors was the pioneer of the modern airline industry that had been Las Vegas's first airline: Western Air Express. One of the factors that helped to decimate the ranks of air carriers arose partially from the impact of the McNary-Watres Act of 1930, which authorized Republican postmaster general Walter Folger Brown to reduce the number of air carriers in transcontinental air service to four: United, American, Western Air Express, and Eastern. The legislation's main purposes were to ensure that cargo bays were filled with airmail, to enable the postmaster general to contract with qualified operators, to change the basis of compensation from poundage to mileage and cubic space, and to make negotiation instead of competitive bidding the method of awarding contracts. Yet it also gave the postmaster general considerable power to select which airlines would receive contracts. While Brown denied any wrongdoing, many air carriers, among them National Parks Airlines and Colonial Airlines, protested his policies.

These airlines complained that the government's selection process for awarding airmail contracts was unfair. Others charged that Brown had operated in collusion with United, American, and Western Air Express. The allegations and suspicions of collusion prompted a congressional investigation spearheaded by Alabama Democratic senator Hugo Black, who appointed C. E. McCoy to lead the investigation under Senate Resolution 349.[45]

Accusations about obstruction of the investigation also arose after the mysterious disappearance of subpoenaed documents. In a letter to the accused, Brown's Democratic successor, Postmaster General James A. Farley, expressed his surprise at finding two files, labeled AIR MAIL and MERCHANT MARINE, in a box containing his personal belongings. After dismissing the theory that the files were placed in his box by a careless staff member, he stated: "There remains only one theory, that these official files were surreptitiously placed among my personal papers at the instigation of someone who was engaged in a conspiracy of character assassination." The files in the box were to be destroyed. Farley ended his letter with: "I am delighted to be able to return the official files relating to air mail and ocean mail unscathed by their fantastic experience in the fiery furnace."[46] The senator's findings from the investigation concluded that the postmaster general had engaged in collusion.

Partisan fury notwithstanding, Brown maintained his innocence and articulated the case of government-business collaboration. A former attorney, he was in fact a staunch opponent of unrestricted competition because he was bitterly disappointed with the corruption and disorganization of the railroad system that had led to unnecessary spending and waste. He feared that a similar reckless configuration would plague the airline industry. In a letter to renowned newspaper publisher William Randolph Hearst, Brown wrote: "During the period of my service in the Post Office Department, the Hearst Papers quite consistently approved my policies and methods in building up an economically independent air transport industry, as an aid to business as well as an auxiliary to National defense."[47] Brown ultimately resigned from his position. Before he stepped down, however, he praised the progress the commercial aviation industry had made. In a letter to Republican senator Simeon D. Fess of Ohio, he wrote: "The air transport industry, which has been fostered by generous government aid throughout the administrations of Wilson, Harding, Coolidge, and Hoover, is still dependent for its very existence upon the airmail service. Much progress toward the goal of economic independence has been made, particularly during the last few years. The revenues of airmail carriers derived from passenger and express services have increased from practically zero in 1929 to the rate of $10 million per year at the end of 1933. To you I need not point out its incalculable value in time of national emergency or the essential service which the airmail performs for the business of the country."[48]

Despite Brown's progress in bringing order to the airline industry, his career in politics was over. After reading Senator Black's findings, an outraged President Franklin Roosevelt ordered the cancellation of all airmail contracts and commanded the Army Air Corps to once again transport the mail. This move slashed a significant portion of the airline industry's business and sent airlines, including those in Las Vegas, scrambling for funding.

In 1930, Las Vegas–based Transcontinental Air Transport, more than $2.7 million in the red as a result of poor management and the provisions of the McNary-Watres Act, had to merge with Western Air Express just to stay in business, each carrier remaining separate but operating under one parent company, Trans Western Airlines.[49] Western Air Express had no choice but to agree to the merger or lose 65 percent of its routes and business, the result of a testy meeting between Pop Hanshue and Walter Folger Brown. The two airlines continued operating out of Las Vegas and Boulder City. In 1932, 1,229 passengers traveled from Los Angeles to Washington, D.C., via Las Vegas, Salt Lake City, Denver, Chicago, and New York. One year later, that number increased to 1,596. The second assistant postmaster general, W. W. Hawes, noted:

> CAM-4 fills a very vital and economic need of the Southwest and the west slope of the Rocky Mountains. In the beginning of air mail service, the Post Office Department recognized the importance of a service connecting Los Angeles with the Rocky Mountain region and the industrial centers of Chicago and the East. The intermediate stop at Las Vegas, Nevada permits an outlet for the vast amount of government and private business correspondence and traffic originating from the huge construction work at Boulder Dam, at the same time furnishing rapid air passenger transportation between Los Angeles and Boulder Dam and east to Denver, Chicago, New York, and Washington D.C. There can be no doubt as to the vital need of this service, not only to Los Angeles, Las Vegas and all of the southwestern territory, but also to Salt Lake and eastern business and banking houses.[50]

Despite relatively robust business on the CAM-4 Route, the airline still was losing money. In 1934 Western Air Express had to reduce its fleet to six airplanes and a staff of four pilots. Transcontinental Air Transport experienced the same problem. The airlines were on the ropes. This situation did not bode well for Las Vegas, which faced losing both its airmail and its passenger service. Western Air Express needed a shakeup, so it turned to Alvin Adams, former vice president of National Aviation, a stock brokerage firm, who through a restructuring of management, plus better marketing, brought the airline to profitability. Western Air Express also received a financial boost from FDR's Air Mail Act of 1934.

The Army Air Corps, under Roosevelt, transported the mail for one month after experiencing sixty-six airplane crashes and twelve fatalities because of substandard planes, inexperienced pilots, and bad weather. As a result of these crashes, the Post Office lost money, and its tarnished reputation of poor management of flight safety resurfaced. The tenuous state of the airline industry drew the attention of a young senator named Patrick McCarran (D-Nev.), who realized the industry's potential to become a major source of military and public transportation and recognized the need to reform it. A staunch supporter of aviation long before he was elected to the Senate in

1933, and not the typical Democrat who supported FDR's liberal New Deal programs, McCarran, like the Spanish dictator Francisco Franco, believed the government should partner with organized corporate interests to promote national commercial aviation growth. In his "Message to the National Aviation Forum," McCarran explained this ideology: "Policy calls for the encouragement and development of an air transportation system properly adapted to the present and future needs of the foreign and domestic commerce of the United States, of the Postal Service, and of the national defense, and the regulation of air transportation in such a manner as to recognize and preserve the inherent advantages of, assure the highest degree of safety in, and foster sound economic conditions in, such transportation, and to improve relations between and coordinate transportation by air carriers."[51] He drafted Senate Bill 3187, which called for the removal of Post Office supervision of the airmail industry and instead prescribed a federal aviation commission that would supervise it, serve as an arbiter between the airlines and employees, issue certificates of public convenience (instead of bidding), and essentially remove the industry from politics.[52]

McCarran, questioning President Roosevelt's power to cancel airmail contracts and defending wrongly accused Postmaster General Walter Folger Brown, asked the Senate to remove the airlines from the Department of Commerce and place them under the supervision of a private agency such as the Interstate Commerce Commission. He wrote: "The whole policy of the legislation, the whole spirit of the law initiated by myself in 1934, carried on until it became a law, was that the Civil Aeronautics Authority should be an independent agency."[53] After protracted debate, McCarran's bill was defeated by filibuster because of questions about intrastate and interstate commerce laws.

Congress passed and President Roosevelt signed into law the Air Mail Act of 1934, which gave the postmaster general the power to award mail contracts through competitive bidding, set air routes and flight schedules, and revise and improve flight regulations and pilot standards. The act also gave the Interstate Commerce Commission the power to review contracts, examine accounting books, and regulate the cost of service. With no other government-sponsored agency to transport the mail, Roosevelt called on private air carriers to do so.

But the act forbade bidding by any airline that originally participated in airmail transportation prior to the McNary-Watres Act. So the original airlines—Western Air Express, United, Eastern, and TWA—simply changed their names and then bid for the same airmail routes along with new airlines that were also applying for the routes.[54] Western Air Express, renamed General Airlines, resumed transporting mail on Contract Air Mail Route 4. Brown's vision of government-business partnership was redeemed.

Though the restoration of airmail contracts allowed the old and new airlines to keep their routes, the airlines still lost money because of the depressed economy. To make up for lost revenue, Western Air Express and Transcontinental Air Transport had to invent new marketing techniques, one of which was offering scenic air tours of Hoover Dam and the Grand Canyon. The Las Vegas City Council even allowed the airlines to install slot machines in the Western Air Express Field air terminal. Looking for other ways to increase profitability in its air route structure, in 1937 TWA received approval from the Interstate Commerce Commission to add Los Angeles to its San Francisco–to–Newark route, with Las Vegas as a stopping point.[55] That same year, the city bought out Western Air Express's lease on Western Air Express Field, thus saving the airline money. With new air tour promotions, slot machine revenues, and added savings from the lease buyout, the airline decided to slowly upgrade its carrier fleet to ensure needed revenue for meeting operating expenses.

Despite the economic hard times, technological imperatives during the 1930s led most airlines nationwide, including Western Air Express, to replace their aging fleets of Douglas M-2s, Ford Tri-Motors, and Fokker 10s with larger, faster, and eventually pressurized airplanes. Gone were the days of noisy, cramped passenger cabins on airplanes made of wood and fabric. While that first generation of passenger planes got passengers to their destinations, the new generation was much better. The planes were sleeker and more luxurious, and they far outperformed their predecessors in passenger seating capacity, speed, and comfort. The new generation of passenger planes was also remarkable because the entire development and manufacturing cycle happened in less than a decade.

In 1933 the Douglas DC-1, the first all-metal twin-engine plane, had appeared on airline flight lines. This passenger plane had cabin seating capacity for twelve passengers and claimed a cruise speed of 196 miles per hour, with engines each capable of producing 710 horsepower, with variable-pitch propellers to allow pilots to set the propeller angles to maximize flight efficiency.[56] Compared to its predecessor, the Fokker 10, which flew at a claimed speed of 103 miles per hour and had to make several stops to refuel, the DC-1 revolutionized air transportation because it was made of durable material, flew longer distances without refueling, and hauled more passengers in a shorter time period. In the traveling public's mind, the new planes restored confidence in air travel safety. With new aircraft design and production moving so rapidly, the DC-1 was soon replaced by its successor, the DC-2, which became the workhorse of the airline industry.

The DC-2, which flew faster than its predecessor and carried up to twenty-one passengers, had a different design than the DC-1. According to William Douglas of Douglas Aircraft Corporation, "The original plan called for a bigger fuselage but essentially the same old DC-1 and DC-2 wing. We added five feet to each wing . . . and soon found out that just putting on more wing didn't give us the lift and stability we needed. It was a case of redesigning the wing."[57] When the plane made its debut, airlines, including Western Air Express, placed dozens of orders. This plane was significant to the airlines and passenger travel because it could function well not only in the short-haul market but also in the long-haul arena. Airlines used the DC-2 to fly passengers from Los Angeles to St. Louis, or Seattle to Phoenix. While the DC-2 performed regular flight duties admirably, the aircraft that especially won the passengers' hearts was the DC-3 "Sky Sleeper."

With a soundproof fuselage, two 1,000-horsepower engines, and seating for twenty-one passengers, the DC-3 showcased the future of commercial aviation. Introduced to commercial flight by American Airlines in 1936, and constructed entirely of metal, the DC-3 epitomized the modern passenger plane, impressive to observers and passengers. Historian Roger Bilstein commented on how "the DC-3 unquestionably set new standards of passenger comfort. Its greater speed and higher ceilings [top altitude] permitted smoother flying for passengers."[58] Western Air Express, Las Vegas's premier airline, bought two DC-3s with "Sky Lounges"—fourteen large, comfortable swivel chairs with plenty of legroom—for use on its Los Angeles–Las Vegas–Salt Lake City routes.[59] In addition to its comfort, the DC-3 was much more fuel-efficient than its predecessors and could travel longer distances without refueling. Including fuel stops, a passenger now could travel from coast to coast in fewer than sixteen hours.

In its advertisements, Western Air Express touted its "Main Liner" service, a DC-3 from Las Vegas to New York. This new generation of passenger planes had a significant impact upon the Southwest, especially Las Vegas. Historian Roger Launius noted that "the aeronautical technology revolution of the 1930s, especially manifest in the Boeing 247 and Douglas DC-3, all-metal, multi-engine transports—allowed a much more rapid and sustained expansion of aviation in the [Southwest] region along essentially the same course that had been started by the early aviation promoters of the Southwest."[60] With DC-2s, DC-3s, and Boeing 247s bringing more passengers to Las Vegas, and construction of the Hoover Dam attracting as many as 300,000 tourists annually, the city's future seemed destined to boom.

To increase its clientele of tourists and gamblers, in spite of the fare increase, the Las Vegas Chamber of Commerce launched an aggressive marketing campaign advertising the city as one of the world's premier resort destinations. With a $75,000 annual budget ("publicity fund"), the chamber hired outside public relations agencies to design advertising layouts. The advertising yielded impressive results. In August 1936 Chamber of Commerce secretary Oliver Goerman reported that 52,357 visitors came to Las Vegas by airplane and automobile, a 9 percent increase over the previous year (47,946).[61] More flights and larger passenger planes bringing more tourists and gamblers to Las Vegas all underscored the need for a larger airport.

As the airline industry steadily grew, especially in Las Vegas, airport officials realized that Rockwell Field, with its short runways and small passenger terminal, was becoming inadequate to handle larger planes and more passengers. This was a common problem nationwide, as a 1936 Works Progress Administration report pointed out: "The airport program looks to the needs of the future. With air travel growing by leaps and bounds in the United States, the fields of today will be inadequate tomorrow."[62] In Las Vegas, Mayor L. L. Arnett and the local Chamber of Commerce began searching for another location.

Mayor Arnett and Chamber of Commerce members R. W. Martin and K. O. Knudson met with Peter Albert Simon, a Texaco fuel distributor and local entrepreneur who coincidentally had been constructing an airport eight miles northeast of Las Vegas to serve as the base for Nevada Air Lines, a regional company that failed to raise the necessary operating funds. In November 1929, Simon struck a deal with Hanshue, agreeing to lease the airfield for twenty years and rename it Western Air Express Field. The mayor, Chamber of Commerce members, and Hanshue breathed a major sigh of relief, because had Simon not agreed to lease his airfield to Western Air Express, Las Vegas would have lost its major airline, and that would have dealt a significant blow to the town's economy. Western Air Express Field emerged during the next decade as the city's airport. But by 1930, with Western Air Express Field annually handling more than 30,000 passengers, and the nation's airports more than two million total, air traffic and airport congestion raised concerns as far away as Capitol Hill about adequacy of the air travel and traffic system, as well as ensuring passenger safety.

With the increasing growth of the airline industry in the late 1930s, the extra workload and pressure of overseeing it proved to be too much for the Department of Commerce. Concerns about airline system inefficiency and safety surfaced, fostering government consensus that rather than being farmed out to agencies such as the Department of Commerce, the Interstate Commerce Commission, and the Post Office, the growing industry needed its own regulatory supervision under a single newly designated government agency specially equipped to handle the task. In 1937 President Roosevelt appointed a committee headed by Senator Patrick McCarran and Democratic Representative Clarence Lea to investigate placing the airline industry completely under the control of the Civil Aeronautics Authority, entirely housed in the Interstate Commerce Commission. In 1938 Congress passed the McCarran-Lea Bill, also known as the Civil Aeronautics Act, and President Franklin D. Roosevelt signed it into law. The bill created a five-member panel headed by an administrator whose task was to regulate airmail rates, airline fares, and routes. The Civil Aeronautics Board (CAB) also was required to establish civil airways, provide better and more-efficient navigation facilities, and establish air traffic control in locales where air traffic was heaviest. Finally, the bill mandated inspection and improvement of the nation's airports to meet the needs of both commercial and general aviation traffic.[63]

The Civil Aeronautics Act was a remarkable success. Senator McCarran noted in a memorandum: "Not a single accident this winter, in spite of an increase in service. In December 1939, the scheduled airlines flew more miles than ever before in their history—a ten percent increase, and December is usually their worst month. The industry's service to the country was better than ever before, thanks to the C.A.A. and the Congress who made it possible."[64] Unlike the Air Mail Act of 1934, which allowed competitive bidding, the Civil Aeronautics Act awarded certificates to airlines through noncompetitive negotiation. With the help of the federal government, McCarran hoped, the airlines would make a profit and become self-sustaining. He noted, "Present indications show that they [the airlines] will probably make a profit of about three to three-and-a-half millions in the calendar year of 1939. It is the hope of the C.A.A. that they will soon become self-supporting, that the Government can reduce airmail subsidies and make a profit of the airmail service."[65] In the same "Message to the National Aviation Forum," McCarran was directly critical of the McNary-Watres Act of 1930 and the Air Mail Act of 1934: "In properly regulating the airlines as to rates, issuance of certificates, and its other economy regulatory functions, by supervising all activities of the airlines, thus prevented the use of unfair business practices and unfair methods of competition. Thus it became apparent to the industry that it had protection, that it could expect justice from the government, and that therefore it could make long-range plans."[66]

The Air Commerce Act gave the government the basic tools it needed to regulate the commercial aviation industry, but the Civil Aeronautics Act was more comprehensive, far-reaching, and rigorous in maintaining air safety standards. In a speech to the National Aeronautics Association at its national convention in New Orleans, Senator McCarran said, "If commerce by air in America was to keep pace with other countries, nothing short of an independent agency, untrammeled by bureaucratic ties of any kind, should come into existence with Federal sanction, so that the industry and science of aviation would grow and prosper under regulation by which that industry and that science would be fostered, promoted, and encouraged."[67] This regulation also applied to airlines serving Las Vegas.

With Western Air Express offering four daily flights between Los Angeles and Salt Lake City, and other commercial airlines such as Transcontinental Air Transport entering the market flying larger passenger planes like the Douglas DC-3, airport expansion was critical. Senator McCarran especially recognized this: "Don't let anyone tell you we are not going to have an airport in Las Vegas of a high standard. Airports are just as much a part of aviation as the planes themselves. Air travel and commerce are here [in Las Vegas] to stay and only are in their infancy."[68]

In 1938 Clark County officials, using New Deal funding, offered to buy out the remainder of Western Air Express's lease on Western Air Express Field. Fearing that it would lose its dominance as the major airline serving Las Vegas because the county would move the airport closer to town, Western Air Express blocked the deal. This left airport officials in a dilemma and with few options. They needed a new airfield and the county did not have enough funds to purchase new land to build an airfield with runways, taxiways, and a terminal closer to town. Its only option was to purchase an already existing airfield, which presented a challenge, because the county had only enough funds to purchase the remainder of the lease for Western Air Express Field. Desperate for funding, county officials looked to Washington for help. Western Air Express Field was literally on the verge of closing, a potential disaster for the airlines and the city. But once again the federal government stepped into the breach, this time in order to advance the nation's preparedness for global war. Aerial combat had made its debut in World War I, but at the time it had not ranked as a strategic priority. Once war broke out for a second time, however, the U.S. Army surveyed the country for suitable aviation training grounds.

The Army Air Corps quickly trained its sights on the Southwest. The region was sparsely populated, geographically expansive, and far enough inland to avoid a foreign attack. Also it had better weather than many other regions where the Air Corps could train its pilots to take off and land safely, and hold practice bombing runs in unpopulated desert areas. Las Vegas was on the list of potential candidates.

An outspoken critic of the liberal welfare state, Senator Patrick McCarran embraced the military-industrial complex. Seeing an ideal opportunity to provide defense for city residents, boost the city's economy through population expansion and increased consumption of goods, and most importantly, upgrade the airport using military funds, the senator used his political power to convince the army to build a base in Las Vegas. On October 5, 1940, the army decided that Las Vegas would be a suitable location to build an airport and train gunnery pilots. Meeting with city officials, on January 25, 1941, the Corps signed a lease to make Western Air Express Field its base and share the airport with the commercial airlines. Part of the agreement allocated $340,000 from the Civil Aeronautics Board for airport improvements that included one 4,000-foot east-west runway, a 5,900-foot north-south runway, a third landing strip, grading, drainage, and hangars.[69] Less than two weeks later, Senator McCarran procured $404,223 in WPA funding for "clearing, grading, surfacing, fences, installation of a water system, electrical facilities, and landscaping."[70] The addition of military airplanes meant more air traffic congestion, never a desirable situation, but airport officials were willing to temporarily put up with the increased air traffic because they badly needed funds just to maintain the airport.

By war's end, the infusion of more than $1 million had helped airport officials reinforce and lengthen the airport's runways to accommodate larger planes. They were also able to build better taxiways and a proper drainage system on the airport apron. With larger and faster passenger planes such as the Douglas DC-4, the Lockheed Constellation, and the Lockheed Electra transporting thousands of people to resort cities throughout the Southwest, including Las Vegas, the Air Corps funds played a decisive role in determining the future of Las Vegas.

Numerous obstacles still stood in the way of development in Las Vegas. Air traffic control towers in their infancy state had only visual control of airplanes in airport traffic patterns. They lacked radar equipment to control planes in other phases of flight. Essentially, Western Air Express Field still was underfunded, and under-equipped to safely handle a large volume of air traffic. And while the Civil Aeronautics Act provided greater regulatory supervision over the commercial air travel industry, and mandated proper facilities for safe aircraft navigation and airport operations, it faced challenges in handling the growing numbers of the traveling public who were boarding more passenger planes than ever before—including those of Western Air Express and TWA to Las Vegas, where lavish new resorts like the El Rancho and Hotel Last Frontier attracted thousands of passengers from distances as far as Chicago and New York. In order to lure people from the East Coast, the airlines had to ensure that the public viewed air travel as safe—which they accomplished by flying new airplanes made of better materials and hiring pilots with more experience. Finally, private airlines struggled to continue offering available flights as airplane fleets and pilots were called to assist with the war effort.

Just as the airlines began to recover financially from the tumultuous 1930s, a new challenge arose with the nation preparing for war. The Department of Defense needed pilots and airplanes to deliver military personnel to various posts in the United States before they went overseas, and military leaders turned to the airlines for assistance.

Despite these challenges, nearly two decades of technological innovation in the aviation industry and government-business partnerships ensured that Las Vegas would have a bright future. W. W. Hawes's explanation about the government-business relationship aptly applies to the airline industry in later years, and even decades. He noted that "Western Air Express has played an exceedingly vital part in American business and industry to the point it has increased its tempo in the rapid transportation furnished by air transport operators as a necessary part of life. . . . American business and the American people cannot do without the advantages of air transportation, both from a passenger standpoint and from a mail and express angle."[71] His observation not only accurately characterized how important air travel was to Las Vegas's economic survival at that time, but foreshadowed how vital it would become, especially in the postwar years when more people would travel nationwide on larger and faster airplanes. The passenger plane would play a major role in the transformation of Las Vegas into a world-class tourist resort city in the desert. The transformation would reveal itself visibly during the postwar years, as larger casino-resorts were built. The jet airplane appeared, and the passenger volume at Western Field (soon to be rechristened McCarran Airport) surpassed a million. The tourist growth came so fast and furious that it caught airport and city officials unprepared. But before Las Vegas could address the issue of rapid growth, the city, its airlines, and the federal government had to prepare for the coming global war.

CHAPTER TWO

A Symbiotic Relationship Forms

*W*orld War II brought dramatic changes to the government-aviation partnership. During the war, government intervention in the U.S. economy reached unprecedented heights. While production remained in the hands of private companies, the government's Office of War Mobilization set prices and ambitious production quotas. Consequently, as historian David Kennedy noted, in 1943 the Allied Powers' aircraft production outnumbered the Axis Powers' production nearly four to one (151,761 to 43,100). "Such figures," Kennedy added, "disguise the fact that the Anglo-American totals include a large number of heavy four-engine bombers, so that Allied superiority is even more marked when the number of engines or the structure weight of the aircraft is compared with Axis totals."[1]

The government's policies sustained a profound impact on commercial air travel. With President Roosevelt's call for the annual production of 50,000 military planes, the production of commercial airline passenger planes by Boeing, Douglas, and other manufacturers came to a halt. Assembly lines turned out B-17 and B-29 bombers in mass quantities, leaving DC-2 and DC-3 assemblies idle. The War Department requisitioned 183 of the country's 359 airliners and two-thirds of the airline pilot workforce to transport military personnel and equipment for the war.[2] With the remaining passenger planes, the airlines managed to fly on reduced schedules, transporting mostly war personnel. In 1942, the War Department formed the Air Transport Command to coordinate all air, cargo, and personnel travel throughout the country and abroad, enforcing strict priorities for air travel. First priority went to anyone traveling on White House business; military pilots ferrying planes to the war front were given second priority, military personnel and civilians traveling on war business third, and military cargo fourth. Civilians had to wait on standby with VIPs such as ambassadors, corporate businessmen, and war correspondents taking precedence. Even in a primarily tourist city such as

Las Vegas, travelers had to be ready to be bumped at any time to give space to someone of higher priority.

After Japan's attack on Pearl Harbor, Western Air Express Field in Las Vegas was immediately activated as a full-fledged military air base, with a name change to Las Vegas Army Air Field. As a joint military and civilian airfield housing fighter planes, small gunnery pilot training planes, and commercial airline passenger planes, as well as a destination for civilian crews delivering Boeing B-17 bombers to the U.S. Army Air Corps, the airfield saw its civil and military operations fall under strict wartime travel priorities. According to Vern Willis, Las Vegas station manager for Western Air Express, "These B-17 bomber ferry crews had the second highest priority for transportation and regularly bumped our passengers off the Western flights to return to their bases. . . . Passengers were patriotic but sometimes felt this was overdoing it. We had to make arrangements to send our passengers on their way by either train or bus."[3]

The country became well aware of the sacrifices needed to support the war. Leisure travel by car, train, or plane was strongly discouraged, but heavy military passenger volume kept the airlines in business with filled flights. Airlines reported 80 to 90 percent of their seats filled, and nationwide, they transported more than 4 million passengers.[4] Americans were on the move with the war effort, crossing the continent to work in the hundreds of defense plants, to train at the many new and old military bases, and to take to the skies for transport to new war regions around the world. Never before that time in the nation's history had so many planes transported so many people. In 1945, the end of the war opened the skies for new airlines and more than five hundred passenger planes, and 6.7 million Americans were eager to fly.[5]

Las Vegas became a wartime city, though it was different in size from the giant military and industrial centers of Los Angeles and San Diego. It was home to an active military base, and to the biggest magnesium factory in the nation. Basic Magnesium Incorporated (BMI)—built near the Hoover Dam with an ample supply of water and electrical power for production, a workforce of 6,500 people, and a peak payroll of $1 million per week—by 1945 had shipped 166,322,685 pounds of magnesium ingots to West Coast defense plants that manufactured airplane cockpits and bombs. The 13,000 BMI construction workers, and the 6,500 factory workers along with their families, brought much-needed new business to Las Vegas with their purchase of goods and homes, and their paying of taxes. The more than 8,000 military personnel and their families stationed at the air base also increased local

business.[6] As a result, the combination of factory workers, military personnel, and federal wartime spending brought the city an economic boom. Las
Vegas historian Eugene Moehring observed: "The effects of wartime spending were magical. Within four years, the town's physical plant and housing
supply had expanded enormously, laying a powerful base for the postwar
years when a vibrant resort economy would team with Cold War spending
to produce a substantial metropolis."[7] All of this growth along with a rapidly
expanding wartime tourism industry underscored the city's need for more
houses and better water, sewage, telephone, and electrical systems. The city
also needed larger hotels and casinos.

Mayor L. L. Arnett, Chamber of Commerce president Bob Kaltenborn,
Chamber of Commerce secretary Robert Griffith, and automobile dealership
owner James Cashman looked to wealthy Southern California real estate
developers and businesspeople seeking to buy cheap land and build resort
hotels. As a major defense, tourism, and hotel industry center in the West,
Southern California contained many businessmen looking to expand their
wealth by taking advantage of the rapidly growing wartime tourism industry
in southern Nevada. One such businessman was Thomas Hull, an affluent,
successful, and widely respected Southern California motel chain owner who
was invited to survey Las Vegas land and consider building a new property
there. To avoid paying higher taxes, he chose 33 acres of property for $150
per acre outside the city limits, near busy Los Angeles Highway 91.[8] He hired
a prestigious Los Angeles architectural firm to design a spacious, sprawling
hotel with a Spanish mission style that was popular in Los Angeles to attract
Southern California tourists. The El Rancho Vegas opened in April 1941 as the
first high-class hotel of the new generation of resorts on the Strip. The desert
resort advertised fine dining, air-conditioning, and a cool swimming pool on
its giant road sign that was designed to catch the attention of overheated
travelers. Selling service and convenience, it offered lodging, parking, restaurants, horseback riding, shops, and an opera house showroom for top-notch
entertainment to attract large crowds and wealthy gamblers. The casino was
small by today's Las Vegas standards, but completely furnished for gambling,
a model for future casinos.

That same year, Southern California contractors Marion Hicks and John
Grayson built the Mexican-themed El Cortez casino-resort on downtown
Fremont Street. This new hotel contained a large gambling casino, fifty-nine
rooms, a restaurant, a showroom, and nicely maintained grounds. While the

El Cortez was a smaller property than the El Rancho Vegas, it was the first major resort on downtown Fremont Street.[9]

In October 1942, theater chain owner R. E. Griffith and his architect nephew, William J. Moore, opened the Last Frontier, located south of the El Rancho. Styled in western frontier design, the property contained a large main building with a casino, showroom, restaurant, and a few bars. Several low-rise buildings consisting of 107 rooms were attached to the main building, which was surrounded by beautifully landscaped grounds. Front sundecks and a large pool attracted passing visitors. The inside was extravagant—walls covered with stuffed animals, lighting fixtures in the shape of large wagon wheels, and a banquet room for six hundred guests. Visitors were offered horseback and stagecoach rides. With a showroom seating six hundred, a parking lot for four hundred automobiles, a whole frontier village filled with authentic historic Nevada ghost town buildings, and original western artifacts for viewing, everything was bigger and better than the El Rancho Vegas.[10]

These new properties certainly were larger and more luxurious than their predecessors, indicators of a growing casino-hospitality industry for the city. But there was an ever-present worry—the war was ending and just as business and tourism had declined with the completion of the Hoover Dam when the workers had left, would business and tourism drop again with the closing of military bases and defense plants? The city fathers wondered how they would bring the tourists back. "Las Vegas could have dried up and blown away," said Mark Hall Patton, curator of the Howard Cannon Aviation Museum. "There was nothing here. The Hoover Dam was built, and the Army Air Corps Gunnery School was being phased out. They had to do something. Tourism and flights to get people here were the answers."[11]

After the war ended, and planes and flight crews were fully restored to commercial airline passenger service, the airlines faced a problem: they were woefully unprepared to accommodate the growing number of Americans who wanted to fly. Historian Carlos Schwantes explained: "After more than fifteen years of deprivation during both the Great Depression and World War II, more Americans than ever before had money to spend and a pent up desire to spend it on travel."[12] During the Depression, only leisure and business travelers could afford to fly on airliners. Historian Roger Bilstein noted: "A large number of Americans in the 1930s continued to view air travel as a risky business. At the same time, they enjoyed the prestige of air travel and boasted to business friends about flying in order to keep up business appointments."[13] Working-class Americans with less money had to travel by train or automobile.

When the country went to war and the government spent millions of dollars setting up military bases and war defense plants, the situation changed. Jobs and money became readily available for working families. People left their homes, traveling across much of the country to answer the government's call for workers. But the War Department demanded sacrifice from everyone. Food, gasoline, tires, and other goods were strictly rationed. People were urged to save their money and buy war bonds. When the war ended and the government lifted its wartime travel restrictions, a consumer society emerged, with people purchasing new automobiles and appliances with the money they had saved during the war by rationing spending. And now they also had more vacation time, which they used to travel longer distances across the country, including traveling by plane. Aviation historian Carl Solberg observed: "A month after V-J Day, the War Department abolished its priority travel rules and a horde of civilian passengers descended on the airlines. It seemed as if all of those who had been denied the chance to travel by air suddenly flocked to fly—and the airlines were not ready for them."[14] As a result, hordes of air travelers packed air terminals nationwide, and airlines increased their flight schedules as much as the nation's airports would permit. In 1946, more than 12.5 million passengers took to the skies. By 1950, that number increased to 17 million, the result of advertising, larger hotels, better customer service for hotel and airline reservations, cheaper airfares, and improved passenger planes.[15]

Feeding this frenzy in air travel was the proliferation of advertisements in magazines such as *Travel Holiday, Travel News,* and the *New Yorker,* and in newspapers like the *New York Times.* Airlines such as Pan Am bought magazine and newspaper space showing bikini-clad women and muscular men in bathing suits on some of the world's nicest beaches, pictures of the luxurious passenger planes, descriptions of recommended recreational activities, and of course, attractive airfares. Other airlines, such as Western, sent letters to chambers of commerce.

Advertising its Second Annual Operation Sun Country, Western joined with the chambers of commerce of San Diego, Palm Springs, Phoenix, Las Vegas, and Los Angeles to invite winter-bound residents of thirty-six northern cities served by Western Air Lines (formerly Western Air Express), including Seattle, Yakima, Spokane, Coeur d'Alene, Lewiston, Idaho Falls,

Helena, Salt Lake City, Billings, Casper, and Rapid City, to fly south for a second summer in these cities. The airline formed a promotions committee, consisting of a Hollywood actress and five civic leaders from the chambers of commerce, who visited thirty-six cities, making sixty-nine personal appearances, thirty-eight radio broadcasts, and fourteen television shows, reaching an audience of more than six million people. Each of the "ambassadors" had the opportunity to tell this huge audience about the attractions and accommodations offered to the winter tourist.[16] While direct advertising helped, so did travel agents, who assisted customers with their travel needs. Organizations such as the American Society of Travel Agents helped customers find deals on airline tickets while charging a nominal fee. Aviation journalist Thomas Petzinger Jr. observed: "Entrepreneurs, retired couples, wives of the wealthy—almost anyone could start a travel agency by stocking the *Official Airline Guide* and leasing some storefront space or a cubbyhole in a suburban shopping strip." He added: "Having identified the most appropriate flight for a customer, the agent would then telephone the airline, or multiple airlines, perhaps, in the case of connecting flights—and make the appropriate reservation."[17]

The air travel boom in turn fostered the proliferation of large urban hotels, often owned by well-known chains such as Hilton, Holiday Inn, and Howard Johnson, which appeared everywhere in cities. Some hotel companies, including Hilton, partnered with airlines, offering reduced room rates to air travelers through package deals. Acting on an idea first proposed by President Roosevelt, Nelson Rockefeller, in his position as coordinator of inter-American affairs, gained Pan Am's agreement to create the Intercontinental Hotel Corporation, a conglomerate of national and international hotels serving passengers and flight crews on six continents. To pay for airfare and hotel stays, customers had the option of using credit cards issued by companies like American Express, which advertised "Travel now, pay later." According to historian Peter Grossman, "In the 1950s, Americans fell in love with credit cards. There were two kinds: charge cards for specific stores and companies, and the universal travel and entertainment charge card."[18] The combination of travel advertisements, the hotel industry boom, and the increased demand for air travel presented the airlines with a challenge to quickly develop faster, more comfortable, and more affordable modes of air travel.

The first step was to phase out older planes like the DC-2 and the DC-3 and replace them with newer, faster, larger planes like the seventy-passenger Boeing 377 Stratocruiser and the Douglas DC-6, luxurious pressurized airliners capable of flying at a speed of 300 miles per hour and at an altitude of 30,000 feet. Using money from the sale of their DC-2s and DC-3s to smaller companies, United, TWA, and Western, the three major airlines serving Las Vegas, leased Boeing 377s and Douglas DC-6s with the option of buying them. Passengers flying on these planes enjoyed comfortable seats, ample legroom, and hot meals and beverages served by flight attendants. Airline executives used the new planes especially for long-haul, transcontinental flights from New York and Chicago to Las Vegas, not only to showcase their luxury but also to demonstrate their speed and fuel efficiency to a growing air-traveling public.

With stronger and more durable engines, aerodynamically efficient wings to reduce drag, and the ability to travel longer distances with fewer fuel stops, a Boeing 377 or a DC-6 offered passengers coast-to-coast travel in less than twelve hours.[19] United Airlines advertised flying "fastest and finest" on its DC-6 Mainliner 300 from Las Vegas to Chicago in seven hours and Las Vegas to New York in ten hours.[20] While airlines replaced their older fleets with these newer planes, Western and TWA kept some DC-3s for short-haul flights from San Francisco and Los Angeles to Las Vegas to save money by burning less fuel.

To meet the overwhelming passenger demand, airlines also added more flights and new routes to their schedules. On January 12, 1950, Western Air Lines inaugurated "excursion flights" between Los Angeles and Las Vegas: passengers traveled on the spacious and luxurious seventy-three-passenger Douglas DC-6 Coachmaster.[21] That same year, United Airlines advertised two daily eastbound flights from Los Angeles to New York via Las Vegas, and westbound flights originating in Denver and continuing to Las Vegas via Grand Junction using the DC-6, which cruised at a speed of 327 miles per hour. The introduction of this new service in 1950 increased passenger volume by 33 percent.[22] In 1956 Western Air Lines advertised "Showroom Holiday Mid-Week Flights" specials, offering low round-trip fares from Los Angeles to Las Vegas for $26.80, San Diego to Las Vegas for $27.30, San Francisco to Las Vegas for $74, and Minneapolis to Las Vegas for $140.40. With Western, TWA, and United offering more flights at cheaper fares, new routes, and larger and faster planes, passenger service to Las Vegas from both coasts and Honolulu increased 167 percent.[23]

While the Army Air Corps was in the process of upgrading Western Air Express Field in Las Vegas, in 1942, George Crockett, an aviation enthusiast and flight instructor from Unionville, Missouri, arrived in town seeking land for a dirt airstrip, a flight school, and an air tour business that he intended to open. Prior to his arrival in Las Vegas, Crockett worked as a sales representative for the Stinson Aircraft Company. His job entailed extensive travel, including trips to Las Vegas. While in Las Vegas, Crockett observed the lack of general aviation airports where private airplanes could stop and refuel. At the same time, he also discovered that the federal government was offering lucrative contracts to flight schools to train pilots for the war. He signed a contract with the Department of the Interior to lease 640 acres of land at a rate of $10 per year for twenty years.[24]

If his business was to be successful, he needed more airplanes than the two that he owned—a Waco and a Luscombe. Crockett leased $35,000 worth of machinery, including eight more airplanes, aircraft tools, and other equipment, from Sioux Skyways, a commercial air carrier that had filed for bankruptcy. In order to receive a Civilian Pilot Training (CPT) contract from the government, he needed a hangar, for which he sold three of his airplanes and borrowed $4,500. Crockett literally built his airfield from scratch, spending days grading the airport's gravel runways. He struck a deal to purchase an old construction shack consisting of three adobe walls and secondhand lumber for $1,800 and built a terminal and a hangar. He also had a water tower filled with water, but nothing to pump it with until he acquired an old diesel engine for $1,200 that he could use to pump running water to the terminal. A gas company gave him an old Texaco truck to be used for fueling airplanes.

On January 1, 1943, Crockett officially inaugurated Alamo Field, an airport with three runways, a terminal building, a flight school, a rental car business (U-Drive-It cars), a motel (the Beacon Inn), and a complimentary shuttle service for pilots to get to town.[25] Initially business was slow, but Crockett's acquisition of a Cessna distributorship and his agreement to allow Douglas Aircraft Corporation to sell and deliver aircraft from his airport helped defray the costs and make a profit, which he used to improve his facilities. In 1946 he lengthened his runways, built new hangars, and opened a restaurant. His airfield was billed as one of the finest of its kind in the country, named in remembrance of his ancestor Davy Crockett, who fought at the Alamo.

The word "Alamo" has historically been associated with U.S. security and expansionism. So it was with Alamo Field. In 1946 the army closed its training base and ended its partnership with Clark County. But in 1947, as the Cold War ensued, the newly created U.S. Air Force, with the financial and political support of Senator Patrick McCarran, announced its intention of establishing a permanent base at the old site. McCarran had always been a strong supporter of aviation, especially for national security, but now he had more in mind than a military base. Essential to the nation's defense, he argued, was the opening of international routes to Europe and other continents for American airlines and air travelers. To promote this, McCarran proposed Senate Bill 326, which called for an "All-American Flag Line," a single airline, Pan Am, to offer daily flights to London, while being financially supported by the U.S. government. This would enable Pan Am to directly compete with British airlines for international routes. The British took umbrage at McCarran's proposal and authorized Pan Am to offer flights to London only two days a week. And the British were not the only ones who opposed his idea.

U.S. Secretary of War Henry Stimson penned a letter to Senator Josiah Bailey, chairman of the Commerce Committee, in which he stated: "The cause of national defense will be best served by affording a maximum encouragement of private, competitive enterprise in the international airline operations of this country, rather than by creation of a single chosen instrument to engage in foreign air transportation."[26] McCarran's "chosen instrument" bill never passed, illustrating that not all private-public partnerships were acceptable. But a second McCarran scheme did gain official sanction. One of the most significant achievements of his career involved acquiring $7 million in federal aid for southern Nevada airport improvement projects under the Federal Airport Act of 1946, a bill that he coauthored.[27] The bill, also an incentive for the city and county to become more proactive in airport expansion projects, bounced back and forth between the House and the Senate for much of the year before it finally passed.

McCarran had shown impressive political muscle when, before the war, airlines were still operating out of Western Air Express Field and airport officials became concerned about air traffic congestion and crowded airspace as the Army Air Corps began to move in with the commercial airlines. Following a series of discussions with Pentagon officials and Senator McCarran, Las Vegas mayor Ernie Cragin and county commissioners Harley Harmon and George Albright discerned that Air Force payrolls and supply orders dictated that Clark County should build its own public airport. The airlines supported this move because it enabled them to function out of their own airport without having to worry about colliding with military aircraft in the airport traffic pattern. Moving the airlines also minimized ground delays, including lengthy lines of airplanes waiting to take off. Throughout the war, Western Air Lines, TWA, and United had complained about how military traffic gave them little space in which to operate. So to please both the Air

Force and the commercial carriers, with the assistance of Senator McCarran, the Clark County Board of Commissioners entered into an agreement with George Crockett to purchase his airport for $125,000. In addition to the sale, the county also included in the contract a thirty-year lease for Crockett to remain on the field as a fixed-base operator. After completion of the deal in 1948, Western, TWA, and United relocated to Alamo Field, while the Air Force continued operating out of Western Air Express field.[28]

Preparing Alamo Field for commercial operations was going to be expensive. But Frank Guswelle, chairman of the Board of County Commissioners, was ready for the challenge. The county had $850,000 in federal airport funds of the $1.5 million needed to complete the project. The Board of County Commissioners proposed a $750,000 bond issue to secure the balance. Despite opposition from a handful of disgruntled local residents who felt that the existing airport was adequate and did not want the additional noise of more airplanes flying over their homes, the bond issue passed on May 1, 1947, with most of the city's residents, casino executives, and the Chamber of Commerce agreeing that airport expansion was needed. As the McCarran Airport Dedication Program noted, "Had it not been for Mr. Guswelle, it is entirely probable that the airport project would have fallen by the wayside. He whipped up enthusiasm in many quarters. He begged and he barked. He cajoled and he drove and, when the pace slackened, he flew into the thick of whatever fight was raging at the time. He held meetings with his other commissioners, with the airlines, with the Chamber of Commerce."[29] Development and expansion plans included two 6,500-foot paved runways, one graded runway, 16,100 linear feet of taxiway, 31,100 square yards of loading apron, a 27,750-square-foot building for administration offices, and new airport lighting.[30] On December 19, 1948, the county renamed Alamo Field—it was to be known as McCarran Field in honor of Senator Patrick McCarran. In a tribute to Senator McCarran, the McCarran Airport Dedication program stated: "The senior senator has always been a friend of the air force and the navy aviation programs and has done everything within his power to see that these arms of the national defense are maintained at a high level."[31]

An editorial in the *Boulder City Journal* praised the new airport as "a far cry from the original facilities in Las Vegas which served the daring pioneer pilots of the 1920s. For instance, the first community 'air field' was a strip of desert a few hundred feet long, which was cleared of mesquite and sagebrush in the old fairgrounds area. Today the site is occupied by the city swimming pool." It also recognized how essential a new airport was to the growth and development of the city, declaring "in the modern air age, up-to-date facilities for all types of aircraft are absolutely essential to the growth and prosperity of any community, and more so in the case of a city like Las Vegas, dependent to a large degree on tourist dollars."[32] With the steady increase in air traffic and passenger volume, it became clear to airport officials that within the decade, more airport expansion would be needed.

With a rapidly growing tourism industry served by three major airlines—United, TWA, and Western—Las Vegas began attracting other airlines, one of which was Bonanza, advertised as Las Vegas's hometown airline. Its president, Edmund Converse, a former World War II military pilot, started the airline in 1946 with two small Cessnas offering sightseeing flights to the Grand Canyon. With business booming, in 1950 he acquired five Douglas DC-3s and offered flights to Reno, Tonopah, Phoenix, and San Diego. Wanting to be a greater presence in the Las Vegas market as a competitor to Western, TWA, and United Airlines, Bonanza strategically attempted to increase business during the winter months by allowing passengers to book flights throughout a fifteen-day period to fly round-trip from Las Vegas to Carson City, and from Las Vegas to Reno. Unlike its competitors, Bonanza also offered its passengers a new amenity of calling friends, relatives, or business partners on radio phones during flight for a nominal fee.[33]

On January 1, 1958, the airline took delivery of the first Fairchild F-27, a turbo propeller-driven aircraft. Capable of flying at speeds of 311 miles per hour, equipped with radar for better navigation and radio frequency coverage, and seats for forty passengers, the F-27 revolutionized the propeller-driven aircraft industry. Advertising itself as the first airline to offer turbojet service, Bonanza added the F-27 to its fleet, which brought enormous prestige and a marked increase in business.[34] Better business also brought expansion and change to the company.

Bonanza needed new land leases, a $350,000 hangar to accommodate all of its planes, and a $125,000 administration building with offices. To bypass the expense of a new hangar and administration building, the airline paid $170,000 to move its $150,000 hangar from Reno to Las Vegas, leased land for fifty years at $800 per month, and insured the hangar for $80,000.[35] In spite of financial difficulties in handling its operation, in 1960 Bonanza became the country's first airline to operate an all-turbo-propeller airline fleet, which meant that it had the fastest, safest, and most efficient planes in the propeller-driven passenger plane industry. Although the airline did relatively well, with a passenger load volume of 67 percent (most airlines had a 75–80 percent passenger load volume), it needed to invent a marketing gimmick to increase that figure.

Using the "Bonanzaland" experiment, the airline offered package deals that allowed passengers to fly Bonanza routes during a fourteen-day period for $90, and a thirty-day period for $160. The experiment worked: Bonanza flights were full. In 1961 the airline transported 316,000 passengers, a 24 percent increase over the 1960 volume.[36] While Bonanza, TWA, United, and Western Airlines experienced significant passenger volume growth by offering affordable fares, and received assurances from casino-resort owners that flights would be full, there was another airline experience that would be important to the sustenance and growth of tourism and gambling in Las Vegas: junkets.

Beginning in 1941, junkets, or non-scheduled charter flights, became a growing business in the air travel industry. Nationwide, people boarded charter planes to travel to Orlando, Miami, New York, Chicago, San Francisco, Los Angeles, San Diego, and other popular tourist destinations. In Las Vegas, casino owners saw an opportunity to tap into the junket industry to increase business and profits. So the El Rancho and Last Frontier casino-resorts contracted with private junket operators primarily from Southern California to transport eager gamblers to their casinos. In 1943 more than 1,100 travelers, about 7 percent of the regular passenger volume, flew to Las Vegas on junkets from Los Angeles, Burbank, and other Southern California cities. In 1959 the Las Vegas Chamber of Commerce reported that 151,173 passengers arrived on junket flights, which amounted to about 10 percent of passenger flights from Honolulu, Dallas, St. Louis, Chicago, New York, and other national cities.[37]

Traditionally, junkets were available only to the wealthy. As Mark Skidmore pointed out in his study of the junket industry, "each junketeer was a male over the age of twenty-one, working in a profession where he earned an annual salary exceeding $30,000."[38] Skidmore also noted an additional prerequisite: each junketeer had to establish a minimum $2,500 line of credit with the casino; in return, he received a complimentary hotel room, meals, beverages, and a show ticket. In *Big Julie of Las Vegas,* author Edward Linn described a similar junket excursion in 1960 when a group of doctors, lawyers, and other professionals flew from New York to Las Vegas on a chartered United Airlines Douglas DC-8 passenger jet. At the casino, "each of them spent hundreds of dollars and in return, received coupons for complimentary beverages, a buffet, and show tickets."[39] New casino-resorts such as the

El Rancho Vegas and the Last Frontier, with their luxurious casinos, lavishly appointed rooms, and premier entertainment, were big attractions for wealthy junketeers who wanted to be pampered and entertained, enjoy outdoor recreation in the sun, drink, eat, gamble, and return home satisfied.

In 1942 the Last Frontier bused many of its customers to town from Los Angeles, Phoenix, Tucson, and other southwestern cities. Because highway travel was too slow, the casino switched to airplanes the following year. By contracting with various air charter services in Los Angeles, the hotel was able to transport more people daily. William Moore, general manager and coowner of the Last Frontier, negotiated an arrangement with these carriers that allowed him to offer a package deal that included a room, meals, and transportation to and from the airport. Guests arrived in Los Angeles from Detroit or Dallas on commercial airlines and then boarded a plane operated by a local air charter service to Las Vegas. In an interview, Moore said that the Last Frontier pioneered charter airplane promotions advertising air service to Las Vegas from other West Coast cities like Los Angeles, Long Beach, and Burbank. This junket air service developed a new niche in the Las Vegas air travel market that "attracted a lot of people" to town.[40]

One of the air services in Southern California with which the Last Frontier contracted was Los Angeles Air Service (LAAS), owned and operated by a young entrepreneur named Kirk Kerkorian. Forced to drop out of school to help with the family farm after his father experienced financial hardship during the Great Depression, Kerkorian had always had a passion for aviation. Having saved his money, he was able to acquire a car-wash business, and in his spare time he took flying lessons. After earning his commercial pilot's license, Kerkorian sold his business and flew airplanes from Canada to England.[41] Later, with experience as an Air Force instructor in the war, Kerkorian thought about starting his own air service. With part of the revenue he had earned from his car-wash business, he set up his new air service with a $5,000 single-engine Cessna to be used for flight instruction and charter flights. He later purchased a Douglas DC-3, a twin-engine Cessna, and a single-engine Beechcraft. In 1950 Kerkorian moved his operation to the Lockheed Air Terminal in Long Beach to compete with forty other junket airlines for business. He struggled for a while until he pleased his customers by upgrading his service with a four-engine Douglas C-54 and spent $28,000 to retrofit it and refurbish the interior.[42] In 1959 he changed the company's name to Trans International Airlines, transporting regular customers and military personnel on a Douglas DC-8 turbojet, and in 1968 he sold the business to Transamerica Corporation for $104 million.[43] Kerkorian had become an important junket operator in Las Vegas, but he wasn't the only one.

Warren "Doc" Bayley, a farmer from Platteville, Wisconsin, had no experience running an airline. Before he became co-owner and chief executive officer of the Hacienda Hotel in Las Vegas during the hotel boom in the late 1940s and early 1950s, he traveled throughout the United States as a syndicated columnist, writing articles about his experiences in various hotels. From his observations, he made special notes of "the good points" to be incorporated into his future hotel—details such as friendly staff, fresh bath towels, clean bed linens, and working air conditioners. Bayley had always dreamed of owning a hotel, and his opportunity finally came while he served as chairman of the board for Standard Motels Incorporated, a West Coast hotel chain.

In 1955, with profits from a fruitcake-manufacturing business in Southern California, Bayley opened a chain of hotels under the name Hacienda Resorts in Fresno, Bakersfield, and Indio, California. That same year, seeking to invest in Las Vegas, he formed a partnership with the National Corporation, a Texas firm that had already begun construction on a property in the city named the Lady Luck Hotel.[44] Just before the hotel was completed in 1956, Bayley, as majority owner, changed the name Lady Luck to Hacienda, sent out initial public stock offerings to stockholders of Hacienda Motels, and received a promising response. But when Nevada Gaming Control Board chairman Robbins Cahill claimed that the Strip was overbuilt and nobody would pay any attention to the Hacienda, stock interests dropped dramatically and the National Corporation pulled out of the partnership.[45] Bayley had to sell his fruitcake-manufacturing business in California to buy the Hacienda. In April 1956 the Hacienda Resort, nicknamed "Hayseed Haven" because it was not a fancy hotel and catered to working-class people, opened, showcasing an Olympic-size Z-shaped swimming pool, room accommodations for 266 guests, and a $17,000 mini racetrack for go-carts, along with annual national competitions.[46]

Bayley shuttled travelers from the airport to the hotel on air-conditioned buses. Upon their arrival at the Hacienda, guests received $5 in gaming chips, a buffet dinner, a bottle of champagne, membership to a golf course lit at night (where each guest had a chance to win $5,000 for a hole in one), and a ticket for a show at the New Frontier (a casino-resort in which Bayley had purchased a 90 percent share and offered to sell the rooms to investors for $10,000 each, an idea that never panned out).[47] Guests also received a tote bag with the Hacienda logo as a souvenir of their experience. While at the hotel, visitors enjoyed complimentary glasses of champagne. Even though Bayley offered all of these fine amenities to his guests, the Hacienda had too many empty rooms because it was too far south on the Strip and tourists went to the other hotel resorts.

During the mid-1950s, as Las Vegas became a more upscale city, attracting affluent tourists and gamblers, room occupancy reached 100 percent capacity, especially on weekends. The New Frontier, Riviera, Flamingo, Tropicana, and El Rancho Vegas offered "Show-time Holiday" room rates for $30, which included three days and two nights at any of the hotels, breakfast, cocktails, dinner, shows, a bottle of champagne, and ground transportation between the airport and the hotel.[48] This public relations program was so successful at filling the Strip hotel rooms to capacity that there was no need for junket travelers, who were turned away. Henry Price, owner of a junket air carrier in Burbank, presented Bayley with the idea of flying in working-class Southern California gamblers and tourists instead of the high rollers, and then busing them from McCarran Airport to the Hacienda Hotel. Bayley accepted Price's offer and scheduled flights on weekdays as well as weekends. Hacienda Hotel general manager Richard Taylor recalled Bayley saying, "If thirty-two people in Los Angeles are willing to fly to Las Vegas on a weekend, then there certainly must be thirty-two more willing to come on a weekday."[49]

Bayley's flight reservations were so consistently filled that he contracted with Price to become the flight services manager of the Hacienda's newly leased Douglas DC-3s. Weekday and weekend junket passenger flights became so popular that Bayley added a large DC-4 to his fleet with profits from the Hacienda. He spent $95,000 of his own money to refurbish that aircraft with comfortable seats and a piano bar and hired former Hollywood actor Dick Winslow as his in-flight entertainer.[50] Winslow played tunes and sang popular songs during the flights, mainly to calm nervous passengers who had never flown before (a common problem in the late 1950s and early 1960s). Other "shows" on these flights featured attractive young women modeling fashions for the mainly male passengers. Contrary to rumor and claims in the book *Green Felt Jungle,* the ladies never performed stripteases, though they did wear lingerie that was considered risqué at the time.[51]

Because of the growing popularity of his flights, Bayley increased the size of his fleet to two Douglas DC-3s, each capable of seating 32 passengers, one DC-4 for 77 passengers, and five Lockheed Super-Constellations that seated 80 passengers each. His additions were timely. In 1959, Hacienda Airlines delivered more than 70,000 passengers to McCarran Airport. In 1960 it delivered 120,000 passengers, and one year later, 170,000 passengers. For 1962, the airline projected transporting 220,000 passengers. These numbers were competitive with the total number of passengers transported by United, Western, Bonanza, and TWA. According to hotel manager Taylor, Bayley's flights were so popular that customers had to book their reservations three or four weeks in advance.[52] The reasons for Hacienda Airlines' success were its catering to working-class tourists, offering low fares, excellent customer service, and frequent advertisements in Los Angeles newspapers and on highway billboards.

To promote his air service, hotel, and rates, Bayley's innovative management team came up with the idea of printing flight schedules on the inside of matchbook covers that were dispensed from cigarette vending machines all across the West. This gimmick was an ingenious promotion tactic. Another advertising opportunity presented itself when construction work on Highway 58 in Victorville, California, created a bottleneck that caused a traffic jam. Bayley paid two attractive females to stand alongside the freeway and hand out flyers to the immobile drivers advertising the Hacienda's junket flights and including coupons for one free buffet at the Hacienda Hotel.[53]

The resort's flight schedule and range of destinations was impressive. Hacienda Airlines offered flights from Los Angeles, Long Beach, Santa Ana, Burbank, San Francisco, and San Diego to Las Vegas using Douglas DC-3s for a round-trip fare of $35.50. Longer-range flights from Dallas, St. Louis, Chicago, New York, Detroit, and Honolulu, at a price of $44.50 round-trip, required use of Bayley's DC-4s and Super Constellations.[54] In a 2000 interview, Boyd Michael, Hacienda's chief pilot and director of pilot training, outlined a typical weekly crew schedule to illustrate the size of Bayley's operation and how it competed with the major airlines in many of the same cities. He recalled that on a Friday afternoon, a Douglas DC-4 crew would leave Burbank Airport for Las Vegas, continue to St. Louis, and terminate in Chicago. The crew had a layover on Saturday, and then on Sunday would leave with a partial load of passengers from Chicago to St. Louis. They then flew to Las Vegas to drop off some passengers and load others. In Las Vegas they switched flight crews and completed the trip in Honolulu. According to Michael, a DC-3 crew flew five round-trips per day between San Francisco and Las Vegas. By 1961, Hacienda Airlines ran seventy flights a week.[55]

Bayley soon found himself the owner of a sizable junket airline. Early in 1961 he ordered twenty-five additional Lockheed Constellations from TWA. The transaction also included thirty-eight engines, twenty-five extra propellers, and $3.5 million worth of spare parts and tools. At that time it was the largest purchase by any air service operator in Nevada history and would have put the value of his fleet much higher than the later appraisal of between $1 million and $2 million. But Bayley began having airline operating certification problems with the Civil Aeronautics Board.

In 1960 he had applied for an operating certificate, but the application was lost under a stack of CAB paperwork and found two and a half years later. Its absence meant that he could not take delivery of the Constellations he had ordered. TWA, Western, and United, the three major airlines serving Las Vegas, out of resentment of the Hacienda's success with the junkets, filed complaints with the CAB accusing Bayley of engaging in unfair competition. The airlines charged that Bayley's airline was operating without a certificate, which was illegal. They also filed a complaint against the Dunes resort, which offered free flights in its Douglas DC-3, alleging that the Dunes operation also lacked a certificate. To be certified as legitimate by the CAB, anyone wanting to transport passengers by air charter had to fill out an application, draft a business plan, and have the documents reviewed and approved by the CAB. To avoid expensive litigation, the Dunes canceled its air service, and Hacienda Airlines became the next CAB target.

On August 12, 1961, a year and a half after Bayley launched his airline, the CAB issued an order to shut it down. CAB examiner Richard Walsh's investigation concluded that Bayley's airline violated federal aviation regulations by operating "package tours" without an operating certificate. Despite the efforts of Hacienda's attorneys and numerous appeals, the courts sided with the CAB and the commercial airlines. Hacienda general manager Richard Taylor argued that the Hacienda had applied for a certificate and had generated a tremendous amount of business for Las Vegas, a point that the resort's attorneys and promoters emphasized. But the argument was futile. Civil Aeronautics Board attorney Robert Toomey argued that if the Hacienda were allowed to operate without a certificate, other resorts would try to follow suit. He asserted that an increase in competition would be detrimental to the big commercial airlines, indicating that the CAB caved in to the political pressure of the major airlines.[56] On July 10, 1962, Bayley was forced to shut down his airline.

None of the other casinos supported Bayley; rather, they sided with the commercial airlines. Casino executives criticized Bayley for targeting middle- and lower-income customers rather than high rollers. They claimed that wealthy people traditionally spent more money gambling and were more representative of the type of image the resorts were promoting. One anonymous casino executive pointedly asked: "What incentive will the airlines have to boost Las Vegas when we fly a minimum of three thousand passengers a month for free?" He further cautioned: "We are also going to be in trouble if we couple booze with gambling and gimmick-style promotions and toss in $5 for lure. . . . That puts us in a class of 'Sin City USA,' an identification we have successfully avoided for five years"—an ironic comment since the city built its reputation around booze, gambling, sex, and promotional come-ons.[57]

Investigative journalists Sally Denton and Roger Morris wrote that it was difficult for Las Vegas to shed its image as "a garish, vulgar place—either too greedy or too cheap, but in any case too much." Nick Tosches, a Las Vegas visitor, called the city "a disease, a nightmare, a paradise for the misbegotten." But for the thousands of visitors and permanent residents, Las Vegas was one of the most attractive and classiest towns in the world, according to Denton and Morris, who wrote, "In only seven years, Las Vegas had become one of the most distinct and showy cities of its kind anywhere on the planet." They also noted: "The city's official handouts extolled its broad streets, ranch-style homes, first-rate schools, eighty-one church groups, four hospitals, and no state income tax."[58] But the growth and development of Las Vegas was not made possible by sex, booze, gambling, nice homes, and favorable tax structures themselves. The airlines also enabled the city to become a popular, modern destination for tourists and future residents who enjoyed the warm weather, affordability of houses, and growing job market.

The controversy over the Hacienda underscored a developing tension between casino executives like Griffith and Hull, who wanted to advertise Las Vegas as a wealthy person's gambling paradise, versus entrepreneurs like Bayley, who wanted Las Vegas to cater to middle- and lower-income guests while also making a profit from gambling and entertainment. Symbolic of upscale Las Vegas, the Flamingo, Desert Inn, and Sahara, more-luxurious hotel resorts than their predecessors, appeared along the Strip, adding to the class-conflict tension. They underscored another conflict: the city of Las Vegas trying to preserve the old Fremont Street hotels and gambling resorts as the last vestiges of the southwestern frontier versus the modern resorts on the Strip bringing in high-class Los Angeles and New York culture and entertainment.

The Las Vegas Chamber of Commerce and prominent downtown Fremont Street casino owners William Moore, Guy McAfee, and Thomas Hull were reluctant to change Las Vegas's image as the last southwestern frontier town. But they could not compete with Mo Sedway and Benjamin "Bugsy" Siegel, Southern California organized-crime businessmen who wanted to replicate luxurious and lavish Southern California Bel Air hotels on the Strip.

In 1946 Siegel, backed by mobster Lucky Luciano and Havana-based Meyer Lansky, opened his dream resort, the Fabulous Flamingo, a property bigger and more luxurious than the elegant Beverly Hills Hotel in Southern California. His original budget of $1.5 million ballooned to more than $6 million, landing him in mortal trouble with the bosses, who suspected Siegel was skimming.[59] The Flamingo ranked as the most glamorous hotel in Las Vegas, with 105 lavishly furnished rooms, a health club, a gymnasium, steam rooms, tennis courts, and areas for squash, handball, and shuttlecock. Behind the main building were stables for horses, a trapshooting range, a large swimming pool, a nine-hole golf course, and several shops. The grounds were landscaped with date palm trees, rare foliage, and exotic species. True to Siegel's desire for class, the whole staff dressed in tuxedos.[60]

Siegel's Fabulous Flamingo represented a significant departure from the El Rancho Vegas, the Last Frontier, and El Cortez with their traditional western decor. The Fremont Street Las Vegans still viewed their town as one of the last frontier towns. A local brochure titled "Las Vegas Nevada, Still a Frontier Town" contained pictures of cowboys, horses, rodeos, saloons, and bordellos.[61] Some visitors stayed at dude ranches scattered outside the town and enjoyed horseback riding, the old frontier game of horseshoes, and other outdoor recreational activities. The El Rancho Vegas, the Last Frontier, and El Cortez offered clean, simple, familiar surroundings and amenities to locals and visitors who were not interested in the luxury, showiness, and big gambling that increasingly characterized resorts on the Strip. Siegel and his colleagues, however, were determined to change Las Vegas's image to that of an elaborate, classy, upscale resort city with luxurious properties that included spacious Monte Carlo–style casinos, well-appointed rooms, air-conditioning, swimming pools, gourmet restaurants, premier entertainment, grass golf courses, and large tennis courts. Everything was designed to attract the wealthy drive-in and fly-in tourists. But effecting such a change would not be easy.

Griffith, Moore, and other Fremont Street casino owners were not yet ready to give up the traditional theme and charm of their community, insisting on continuing to promote Las Vegas as an authentic southwestern frontier town. To prove their seriousness, they paid a local business to construct *Vegas Vic*, a giant cowboy statue famous for waving and saying, "Howdy, podner" to all tourists walking on Fremont Street. *Vegas Vic* was the perfect advertising gimmick for the Old West, appearing in newspaper advertisements, in flyers, and on television, where he was viewed by millions of Americans. But even with this advertising, Fremont Street was no match for the gorgeous hotel resorts on the Strip that attracted wealthy Southern California businesspeople, Hollywood celebrities, world-class entertainers, and enormous crowds. Historian John Findlay noted, "In 1955, the owners of the Last Frontier Hotel turned their backs on the bygone era of the Old West nostalgia and opened their doors to the age of the future. . . . Gone was the Old West theme, replaced by space-age luxury that can be traced in a straight line from Los Angeles to the Strip."[62] Historian Hal Rothman summed up the shift thus: "The 'glamour girl' image replaced 'Vegas Vic' and the western theme used by early properties to portray Las Vegas as a wild, no-holds-barred frontier town. By the early 1950s, Las Vegas's image had more in common with Hollywood than with Dodge City."[63] Like the airlines modernizing their fleets and adding first-class amenities to attract more passengers, the emerging casino-resorts paved the way for bigger and even more luxurious resorts to expand their clientele.

In the 1950s such new resorts proliferated along the Strip, each one striving to outdo the others in grandeur and size. In April 1950 the Desert Inn opened, labeled "the jewel of the resorts" by casino owners and city marketers because of its spaciousness and unique design. With seventeen richly landscaped areas, state-of-the-art entertainment, air-conditioning, gourmet restaurants, a sky room for nightly dancing, and a meticulously manicured and landscaped eighteen-hole golf course, this hotel became the Strip's premier resort.

It was nearly outdone in December 1952, when the Sahara opened as the Strip's sixth hotel. The two-story building boasted 276 rooms, an Africa motif throughout the facility, a luxurious lounge, and a gourmet restaurant. In later years, the Sahara built a "space center," a 4,000-square-foot convention center used for business meetings and special events. That same year, the Sands opened. It became a legendary resort with the popular Copa Room, in which big-name entertainers Liberace, the Rat Pack—Joey Bishop, Dean Martin, Sammy Davis Jr., and Frank Sinatra—and Elvis Presley gave sold-out performances. These world-class entertainers attracted thousands of people from all parts of the country. The giant Sahara casino-resort landscape featured exotic shrubs, palm trees, and luxurious gardens that surrounded a glass-walled restaurant that overlooked its beautifully arbored grounds.

In April 1955 the eleven-story Riviera opened as the tallest building in Las Vegas and the first high-rise hotel in town. Its European design, lavish gardens, multipurpose facilities, and other amenities earned the property the title of "first self-contained vacation community." On May 23, 1955, the Dunes opened as the tenth resort on the Strip. Called the "miracle in the desert," it had 194 rooms, a ninety-foot swimming pool, a fifteen-foot lagoon, a magic carpet revue showroom, and an eighteen-hole golf course. It pampered its guests by offering them complimentary drinks, dinner, and shows. In May 1956 the fifteen-story Fremont hotel opened, replacing the Riviera as the town's tallest building and quickly gaining fame for its gourmet restaurants with world-class chefs. In June 1956 the Silver Palace opened with Las Vegas's first two-story nightclub.

In April 1957 the Tropicana opened with sprawling bungalow-style buildings and a total of one thousand rooms, and one year later, in July 1958, the Stardust opened with a 105-foot pool, a 16,500-square-foot casino (the largest in Nevada), a horseman's park, an area for rodeos, a track for Grand Prix racing, a golf course, and a country club.

In total, hoteliers spent more than $7 million on these luxurious resorts to offer the best accommodations, recreation, and entertainment to all kinds of travelers. Boosters and marketers from the Las Vegas Chamber of Commerce now promoted the city as an elegant, classy, glamorous resort destination. Hired advertising agents peddled the town as a desert paradise for tourists and gamblers. They also billed it as an "atomic city," after President Harry S. Truman approved the creation of the Nevada Proving Ground, the only peacetime aboveground nuclear testing facility in the continental United States.[64] On January 27, 1951, the first atomic test took place. Exploiting the publicity that accompanied the test, Las Vegans began marketing the detonation as one of their city's attractions.

Despite all the money spent on building new casinos, Las Vegas still sat isolated in the middle of the southern Nevada desert, with accessibility to major western cities and more-distant metros across the nation always a challenge. Modern new airlines reaching out across the continent and overseas were beginning to rise to that challenge. With a growing increase in the number of tourists and gamblers coming to stay at the new Strip resorts, and large airline passenger planes such as the DC-4 and the Boeing 377 Stratocruiser annually transporting more than 35,000 passengers to Las Vegas, city officials realized that McCarran Field needed immediate expansion.

Even after a $150,000 program to pave the three runways, provide night lighting, and build an air traffic control tower and weather station, McCarran Airport remained too small for the 35,106 passengers, the 99 daily flights, and the 77-passenger DC-6s and Lockheed Constellations that annually arrived by the late 1940s and early 1950s.[65] As the Sands, Sahara, and other plush resorts appeared on the Strip in the 1950s, passenger volume at McCarran continued to soar. In 1955, more than 500,000 passengers walked through the airport's gates, forcing airport manager Robert Metten and his staff to draw up plans for further expanding runways, taxiways, and terminal facilities. Metten's deputy director and eventual successor, Gordon Miles, also acknowledged that expansion was imminent: "Remodeling the present airport would be good for ten years, but the city will need a new airport in twenty years."[66] By 1957, with more than 700,000 people annually arriving by plane, the crunch proved so great that Metten and Clark County commissioners George Albright, Harley Harmon, George Christianson, and others decided their only recourse was to expand the current airport and build new facilities. As Albright stated in a county resolution, "The existing terminal building at McCarran Field is inadequate for the present volume of traffic. After careful study and research, the Board of County Commissioners has determined it more practical to construct a new building rather than enlarge the existing one."[67]

In 1957 Metten hired contractor Leigh Fisher to conduct a comprehensive airport study. When completed, the study estimated the cost of a new airport to be $3.865 million. Expansion of the existing facilities alone would run $2.5 million (in today's figures, around $5 million).[68] The expansion plan included $600,000 for runway extension and lighting (the east–west runway would be extended from 6,500 feet to 10,000 feet and widened to 150 feet, with high-intensity runway lighting for night flights), taxiway lighting and widening to 75 feet, and two buildings connected by a ramp. The first building would house ticket counters, baggage handling, airline offices, and rental counters. The second building, at 90,000 square feet, would contain twelve gates (with the flexibility to increase to twenty gates), waiting lounges, restaurants, bars, a nursery, concession stands, and restrooms.[69]

Once again the federal government stood ready to lend a helping hand. Approximately 62.5 percent of the expansion cost would be provided through federal grants. The county, however, would still have to float a $5 million bond measure and use all of its resources to pay for the rest.[70] Airline representatives Ralston Hawkins of Bonanza Airlines, Charles Wyre of TWA, R. E. Costello of Pacific Airlines, D. Dodgson of Transocean Airlines, James Keefe of Western Air Lines, and Ed Lupien of United Airlines agreed to the economic soundness of the expansion plan and costs as long as takeoff and landing fees would remain at $.08 per 1,000 pounds of aircraft weight (including passengers, luggage, fuel, and cargo).[71] Getting public approval of the bond measure was another matter.

Initially, the bond issue had few supporters because taxpayers had just voted to approve a $6 million bond issue for local schools, and many felt McCarran Field was adequate for the airlines. Not even all of the city's travel entrepreneurs expressed enthusiasm for the airport project. Some local residents vociferously objected to the entire project, calling it a "white elephant basking in the sun." Local radio host Joe Julian questioned the logic behind moving the airport.[72] Airport director Gordon Miles even recalled the anger of some casino-resort executives when the county moved the airlines to Alamo Field in 1948: "When the airport was on the west side [of town], all hotels felt that the traffic would be diverted away from their hotels."[73] Still, with 959,063 passengers arriving at McCarran in 1959 and the airport handling 99 flights a day with basic air traffic control equipment, most residents, casino owners, and local businessmen, including Herb Waite of Southern Nevada Power Company and Andy Ruckman of the Southern Nevada Industrial Foundation, came to understand that the city needed a larger airport. On November 6, 1957, Waite and Ruckman met with county commissioners Harley Harmon, George Albright, and Arnold Christensen to discuss airport space and leases to expand their businesses. The two business leaders subsequently made a case to the public that the city's economy would benefit from an airport business park. To mobilize additional support, Gordon Miles also mandated that all airport electronic equipment repairs be done by Leonard Sheafer and Gerald Forston, owners of Airborne Electronics, a local Las Vegas business.[74]

Just a few days before the vote on the bond issue, the Las Vegas Chamber of Commerce overwhelmingly endorsed the measure by a vote of 12 to 1 (the member who voted against the measure owned a hotel). One member justified his vote for a new airport this way: "The increase of Las Vegas air travel is dependent on the construction of a new terminal building and other improvements at [the new] McCarran Airport." Another predicted a coming revolution in air transport technology and argued that a new airport was vital "to keep up with the jet age of transportation."[75] The city's leading newspaper also endorsed the airport. *Las Vegas Review-Journal* editor Al Cahlan penned an article in support of a new airport, explaining: "The present facilities are completely unfit for the class of people we are getting to come to Las Vegas, and the increasing number of airlines serving this community has brought obsolescence so far as accommodations are concerned." With more middle- and upper-class visitors coming to stay at the luxurious Strip resorts and Las Vegas wanting to continue bringing in even more, the city needed a new airport. Cahlan continued: "Air travel into Las Vegas has mushroomed to a point where, this year, it is probable that traffic will reach the one million mark."[76] On March 17, 1960, the bond issue passed by a voter margin of two to one. Las Vegas had its newly expanded airport.

Voters' approval for construction of a new airport could not have come at a better time. As some Chamber of Commerce members had predicted in the bond issue campaign, the age of jet travel was soon upon Las Vegas. The new McCarran Airport would accommodate the modern aircraft. According to chief architect John Replogle of Welton Becket and Associates, the new McCarran facilities have been designed for the convenience of the jet-age traveler. "We have tried to provide [the traveler] as efficient service on the ground as he usually receives in the air."[77]

In 1958 airlines such as Pan Am, United, TWA, and American added Boeing 707s, Boeing 720Bs, and Douglas DC-8s to their fleets, luxurious jets with seating for 185 passengers that delivered thousands more travelers to the nation's cities, making even greater profits and sending airport managers searching for funds for airport expansion to accommodate these large jets. They traveled at a speed of nearly 600 miles per hour, shrank geographic distance, and made air travel more popular than ever. The air travel industry was growing so rapidly that airport officials nationwide had difficulty keeping up. They did not have sufficient funds in their budgets to meet the expansion costs, so they turned to federal, state, and local funding. This approach proved to be challenging because Congress was more interested in expanding the nation's highways and roadways through the Federal Highway Act of 1956 than in funding airport expansion projects. As a result, airport officials had to work with what moneys they had, and that was the case in Las Vegas as well.

Since the 1920s, airport expansion and inadequate funding for expansion had been dominant themes. Passengers often complained to airline and airport officials about standing in line for hours at small airline ticket counters, walking through narrow and dimly lit airport concourses to get to the gates, inadequate restroom facilities, and not enough seats at the gates. As aviation historian Roger Bilstein noted: "Airports across the country developed reputations for littered waiting areas, odoriferous restrooms, and packed coffee shops. Jammed passenger terminals seemed the rule rather than the exception."[78] Airport planners and managers also recognized the need for better air traffic control centers and towers to handle the increased air traffic, as well as improved navigation equipment (such as the instrument landing system, or ILS) so pilots could safely fly instrument approaches to airports in inclement weather. The airlines also needed more ticket counter space, baggage carousels, and gates.

With the increased numbers of passengers walking through the terminals, airport officials needed to include in their expansion plans restaurants, shops, and concession stands as other sources of revenue to help pay for expansion costs and day-to-day airport operations. In 1947 commercial airlines had transported more than 10 million passengers nationwide. By 1958 that number exceeded 55 million. An editorial in the *Las Vegas Sun* noted: "Air travel was expanding [at an alarming rate] and the public [increasingly] came to depend on commercial aviation."[79]

After carefully examining the results of the Leigh Fisher study, in 1959 county commissioner Clesse Turner concluded: "The combination of lack of space to accommodate jets [in the future] and a bad airport location made it prohibitive to enlarge the present [terminal] building." This was why the newly expanded airport was vital. He emphasized that "in the next ten years, practically every major airline will have changed over to jets. . . . The feeder lines will have to convert to some sort of turboprops. . . . When that time comes, air traffic will soar enormously."[80] His prediction was correct.

This explosive growth in the air travel industry, the appearance of newer and larger passenger planes, including jets, and the growth and development of the casino-resorts marked the beginning of a new era for Las Vegas. It was a time when the symbiotic relationships among airlines, federal government, casino resorts, and the city strengthened. The years 1941–1958 also marked a time when Las Vegas became a modern city. With a population exceeding 48,000 people, affordable housing, the availability of many jobs (especially mining magnesium, which was crafted into airplane wings that were sent overseas to support the war effort), and large public works programs, including construction of roads, public parks, and schools, Las Vegas permanently shed its past as an obscure little railroad desert town constantly struggling to survive. Its new status as a popular tourist destination annually attracting eight million visitors (in 1955) enabled it to directly compete with larger resort cities like Los Angeles, Orlando, and Miami. As Las Vegas historian Hal Rothman observed, "In the comfortable political and cultural climate of southern Nevada, Las Vegas became the center of gaming in the western hemisphere. . . . Most of the money the casinos won came from visitors, not from local residents. . . . Combined with the technological improvements such as the expansion of McCarran Airport in 1963, the 'dinky horrible little oasis town' that Lansky and Siegel first saw stood poised to take advantage of widespread wealth and changing cultural mores."[81]

Passenger planes played a vital economic and technological role in helping Las Vegas make this transformation. They brought in thousands of travelers from all parts of the country, and casino-resort owners and city officials responded by building a state-of-the-art airport to accommodate the planes and their passengers. But as the passenger volume continued to expand rapidly, larger passenger jets like the wide-bodied Boeing 747 and Douglas DC-10 delivered three hundred passengers per flight, and other jets like the Boeing 727, 737, and the Douglas DC-9 continued to deliver one hundred to two hundred passengers per flight, the new airport quickly became insufficient. Also, in response to the growing demand of passengers, casino-resort executives Kirk Kerkorian, Jay Sarno, Jackie Gaughan, and others built bigger, more magnificent, lavish, and luxurious resort properties, some of which had high-rise buildings with more than 2,500 rooms for guests. The airline industry, the casino resort industry, and the city grew rapidly, and continued to do so for another four decades, keeping airline and airport officials busy with expansion.

CHAPTER THREE

Jets in the Consumer Age

*I*n the history of American aviation, there were two monumental milestones that legitimated and solidified the airplane's future as a viable mode of public transportation. The first was Charles Lindbergh's famous transatlantic solo flight from New York to Paris in 1927, an accomplishment that opened the nation to the age of air travel. The second was Pan American Airlines' inaugural Boeing 707 jetliner flight from New York to Paris in October 1958, launching the airlines and the nation into the jet age.[1]

Jets revolutionized the air travel industry. With their capacity to hold three times as many passengers as the Lockheed Constellation and the Douglas DC-6, their ability to fly nearly double the speed of their propeller-driven predecessors, and their lengthy fuel range, the Boeing 707 and the Douglas DC-8 changed air travel by bringing domestic and international cities closer together through time. Pan Am president Juan Trippe remarked, "In one fell swoop, we have shrunken the earth."[2] Boeing 707s and Douglas DC-8s delivered passengers to Los Angeles nonstop from New York in five hours, less than half the time required for a propeller-driven DC-6 or DC-7. A flight from New York to Paris took eight hours. Yankees looking to take a weekend off in popular Havana hopped flights from New York and Chicago rather than boarding the ferry at Key West.

While the advent of jets symbolized a new age in air travel, it also required airports to undergo considerable renovation. American cities from coast to coast prepared for the passenger jet by building jetports to meet long takeoff and landing requirements and to accommodate the millions of travelers taking to the air from all parts of the nation and the world. Aviation historian Roger Bilstein observed this growth of airports and expanding international business markets, noting: "Immediately after the war, trans-Atlantic flights drew large numbers of American executives seeking new business opportunities in Europe especially during the development phase of the

Common Market when Europeans needed American machinery and products essential to reindustrialization after the war."[3] While market expansion and rapid increase in passenger travel were good for the airlines' business, those developments also meant that airport officials would have to promptly enact expansion plans for airports that were woefully unequipped to handle jets and millions of people. If airports—including Las Vegas—were to meet the needs of airlines and air travelers, they would have to spend millions of dollars on enlarging terminals, reconfiguring airfields, and renovating parking facilities.

Las Vegas welcomed jet passengers by building several luxurious new high-rise casino-resort hotels and a new airport. It is no exaggeration to say that jet travel put the city on the map as an international travel destination along with Seattle, San Francisco, and Los Angeles. Las Vegas historian Eugene P. Moehring noted: "Beginning in September 1960 when United Airlines introduced non-stop service to Los Angeles, Chicago, and New York, jets expanded Las Vegas's gaming hinterland, making the city accessible even to East Coast residents."[4]

Las Vegas had long anticipated the arrival of the powerful new planes. As early as February 1950, speaking to Las Vegas Rotary Club members at a large convention held in the Last Frontier casino-resort on the Strip, Jerry Pettis, executive assistant to the president of United Airlines, announced that U.S. commercial airline corporations were taking a serious look at new jet aircraft being designed at both the Boeing and the Douglas aircraft companies. These jets would eventually replace the propeller-driven fleets in current use. Time and testing were needed to ensure safety before the new jet aircraft would be added to United's fleet. Pettis explained, "The four scheduled airlines serving southern Nevada—United, Western, TWA, and Bonanza—are all striving to improve their service, since tourists using planes have more time to spend at their destinations. Hence, if these airlines bring more tourists into Las Vegas, you residents benefit directly because the visitors stay longer and spend more."[5] In a 1955 address to local civic leaders, Bob Metten, the manager of McCarran Airport, added to the anticipation with the revolutionary words "the jets are coming."[6]

Talk of jets' being added to airline fleets and coming to U.S. cities generated mixed feelings—excitement about the new airliners that would travel at nearly 600 miles per hour, improve safety, and offer more passenger space and nonstop global flights, but trepidation about the enormous cost of acquiring Boeing 707s and Douglas DC-8s. William Hildred, director general of the International Air Transport Association, wrote: "One does not buy a $5 million jet as if it were a new bicycle. Even one jet aircraft necessitates special maintenance facilities, maybe a new base or a new hangar, extensive training of ground and airborne personnel, complete replanning of ground handling facilities, and many other changes in airline organization, all of which begin costing money before the aircraft can be put into service."[7] C. E. Woolman, president of Delta Airlines, also initially expressed skepticism as his airline prepared to buy its first jets: "We are buying airplanes that haven't been fully designed, with millions of dollars we don't have. We are going to operate them off airports that are too small, in an air traffic control system that is too slow, and we must fill them with more passengers than we have ever carried before."[8] But the promises of faster air travel, and the availability of low-interest loans to the airlines from government and private lending firms, were irresistible. Furthermore, greater flight frequency, passenger travel demand, and the possibility of airline profitability would pressure the Civil Aeronautics Board to sanction lower ticket prices (during this time, the airline industry was still regulated by the government, which controlled ticket prices). Competition among the major airlines was another reason for forging ahead with leasing jetliners. By 1965 the value of total passenger jet deliveries to the airlines totaled $1.2 billion, and a decade later it had more than tripled, reaching $3.8 billion.[9]

In 1959 TWA was among the first to add jets to its fleet to compete with Pan American for international transatlantic routes, and later introduced jets in its domestic flights. Western Airlines, with heavy passenger volume through the 1950s from increasing flight routes, grew from a minor to a major airline and soon added jets to its fleet as well. Bonanza Airlines, covering short to medium-length routes, added turbo propeller-driven Fairchild F-27s to its fleet.

The primary advantage of the jet was that its engine, which had fewer moving parts than the piston engine, was more reliable, safer to operate, and easier to maintain. It burned kerosene, much cleaner than gasoline, and it produced tremendous thrust for the weight. Thus jet aircraft could be made larger and could fly faster than piston-engine planes. Though jets had larger fuel tanks for longer hauls than propeller-driven planes, they guzzled hundreds of gallons of jet fuel per hour, making them inefficient and adding to the operating expense. They were, nevertheless, the passenger planes of the future. The Boeing 707s, first to come off the Boeing assembly lines in 1958, and at the same time the Douglas DC-8s from Douglas assembly lines were sleek, stealthy, long-bodied jets capable of flying at altitudes of 30,000 to 40,000 feet, high above the storm levels, and reaching speeds of 575 miles per hour. With seating for 165 to 200 passengers, they had luxurious and spacious interiors with comfortable seats, ample legroom, and like the propeller-driven airliners, a professional staff of flight attendants to assist travelers with their needs.

Recalling his first experience on an American Airlines Boeing 707 jetliner, flying from New York to Los Angeles, Daniel Solon, a transportation journalist, remembered how "the flight attendants made it [the flight] a good party. I know that sounds a little frivolous, but we had a very good time, and five and a half hours later we were on the ground in L.A."[10] Jet cabins were much quieter than the propeller-driven DC-6 and Lockheed Electra cabins, so passengers could enjoy listening to music, or read an assortment of newspapers and magazines. The whole atmosphere of the jet was one of sophistication, inspiring passengers to be cordial, to dress in their best clothes, and to feel privileged to fly. *Fortune* author Paul Lukas wrote: "The Boeing 707 was the single most transformative event in the annals of twentieth century flight. It affected everything from heavy industry to tourism, killed the railroads and ocean liners, while having a cosmopolitan sophistication."[11] An editorial in the *Las Vegas Review-Journal* praised the size and speed of passenger jets: "New jets carry upwards of 100 passengers where the present conventional planes average around 60. The speed of the jets will be so fantastic that a trip from New York to Las Vegas will take only as much time as a jaunt from Denver to Las Vegas does now."[12]

But jets also had their downsides. Among the biggest complaints had to do with their ground noise and engine exhaust. The decibel level of jets taking off and flying over residential neighborhoods with high engine power thrust settings drew the ire of city residents, who vociferously complained about the noise and, in some cases, their homes shaking. T. A. Heppenheimer, an associate fellow of the American Institute of Aeronautics and Astronautics, noted: "When the jetliners entered service, complaints from homeowners were soon as loud as the engines themselves. People were soon bombarding the new FAA and their congressmen with angry letters. The FAA administrator, Elwood Quesada, had to get an unlisted phone number because people were waking him up with phone calls at three and four o'clock in the morning."[13] In Las Vegas, to control noise, airport officials implemented late-night curfews, prohibiting passenger jets from taking off, and they restricted planes from making turns over residential neighborhoods at low altitudes. McCarran Airport even installed special takeoff pads tilted downhill to lessen the sound of jet engine noise on takeoff.[14] McCarran, with more than 128 takeoffs each day in 1963 and surrounded by residential areas, prided itself on being a good neighbor by reducing jet noise as much as possible.

Another drawback of the jet engine was the exhaust that constantly spewed out of the tail cone, adding to city pollution. Even though jet fuel (kerosene and water) burned cleaner than regular aviation gasoline that fueled the radial engines of DC-4s and Lockheed Constellations, which also belched large white clouds of exhaust, residents living near airports complained to airport authorities about the smell of jet exhaust. Airport officials could do little to remedy the situation, though, and the airlines continued to lease more jets.

Edmund Converse, CEO of Las Vegas's hometown Bonanza Airlines, purchased three Douglas DC-9 twin-engine turbojets. The DC-9, which cost $3 million to manufacture and was configured for 75 to 100 passengers, was quieter and faster, and could fly greater distances without refueling than the F-27 turboprop in use at the time. Having a top speed of nearly 500 miles per hour, the DC-9 quickly became a favorite with the traveling public, who could now arrive in Los Angeles from Las Vegas in fifty minutes instead of the ninety-minute flight time of the F-27. With DC-9s now in its fleet, Bonanza put pressure on the highly competitive Las Vegas–to–Los Angeles route by adding ten daily nonstop flights at a round-trip price of $13 to compete with Western's "Thrift Air" flights, which charged passengers $26 to fly round-trip on Douglas DC-6B propeller-driven planes.[15] While Bonanza did not make as much of a profit from these discount fares because Las Vegas was a low-yield, high-volume market, with government funding to replace its DC-3 fleet with F-27s, the airline would be able to operate the F-27s at a lower cost per seat mile as an incentive to help promote the more-efficient modern turbine engines over inefficient radial engines.[16]

The airlines also offered three daily round-trip flights from Las Vegas to Reno and five daily nonstop flights to Phoenix. This addition of more flights drew the praise of Nevada senators Alan Bible and Howard Cannon, who jointly commended the CAB's decision, declaring: "The Board has properly taken cognizance of the fact that the continuing growth of both Las Vegas and Reno fully justifies a commensurate expansion of airline service."[17] Any flight under 100 miles was not economical for the DC-9 because jets operated most efficiently at higher altitudes, faster speeds, and longer distances, so CEO Converse kept F-27s and a few DC-6s for the short hops. In 1967

Bonanza transported more passengers (1,005,193) and generated more revenue ($20,840,000) than ever before in the airline's history.[18]

On July 1, 1961, United, Bonanza, TWA, and Western were joined by a new competitor, Delta Airlines, which inaugurated its service to Las Vegas with a 58-passenger propeller-driven Douglas DC-7 originating in Atlanta with stops in Birmingham, Alabama, and Dallas, Texas.[19] With the help of Nevada senator Alan Bible, Delta filled a badly needed niche for visitors and Las Vegans. Testifying before the Civil Aeronautics Board, Bible said: "It is clear to me this outstanding potential for future development of tourist facilities, the Las Vegas area is peculiarly in need of good air transportation service to all parts of this nation. People of the South and Southeast portions of the country will now be able to come to Nevada and the far west directly. No part of the State of Nevada has ever had good, one-carrier air transportation service to any part of the Southeast."[20] Delta's arrival in Las Vegas was significant because prior to that time, no airline serving Las Vegas had offered passenger service to southern and southeastern cities. A Delta Airlines official observed, "On July 1, 1961, a Delta Air Lines' jet (DC-8) departed Las Vegas, crossed the continent, and opened a new economic highroad between this city and the Southeast. The Las Vegas authority helped mark the transformation of Delta, once a regional carrier, into a transcontinental airline."[21] The new airline boasted a nationwide fleet that included eighteen jets—Douglas DC-8s, Convair 880s—and by 1965 it was an all-jet fleet.

Hailing the airline's new service to Las Vegas, Al Adams, Las Vegas airport sales manager, proclaimed: "With this service, Delta provides an excellent opportunity for people of the South and Southwest to visit Las Vegas and in turn, give residents of Nevada convenient service to do some visiting themselves."[22] The airline's first year in Las Vegas brought a 70 percent increase in air travelers in the Las Vegas market. And on June 1, 1962, Delta replaced its DC-7 with a 200-passenger DC-8 turbojet. In marking the occasion, T. M. Miller, Delta's vice president of sales, stated: "Our flights have done even better than we anticipated. And we are delighted to report that they are profitable for Delta as well as for the Las Vegas tourist industry."[23] The major carriers United, Delta, and TWA were not the only airlines benefiting from jets, however. New regional airlines also began leasing jets.

Regional Airlines

In the late 1960s, because of intense competition for popular West Coast routes, Bonanza Airlines of Las Vegas, Pacific Airlines of San Francisco, and

West Coast Airlines of Los Angeles merged to form Air West, a regional airline. With its Douglas DC-9 jets seating 75 passengers, the airline was in stiff competition with California-based Pacific Southwest Airlines (PSA), Western Airlines, TWA, and United, for the popular Las Vegas–to–Los Angeles, Las Vegas–to–San Francisco, and Las Vegas–to–Portland routes. The new merger set records in passenger volume, with 106,342 passengers at McCarran Airport in the first quarter of merged operations.[24]

In 1969 billionaire Howard Hughes purchased Air West, renaming it Hughes Air West. This was not the first airline he had owned. In 1939 he acquired control of TWA with the purchase of 78 percent of the company's stock, helping the airline to grow and expand its network.[25] With strong financial backing, he consolidated maintenance operations and replaced TWA's older fleet of Douglas DC-2s and DC-3s with beautiful new Lockheed Constellations that he codesigned. While Hughes lacked a college education and had no formal training in aeronautical engineering, he was an aviation genius and an astute businessman. At a young age, he formed his own airplane company, Hughes Aircraft, to build fast planes in which he broke records for round-the-world flights, which ended in ticker-tape parades in New York.

Like his airline competitors United, TWA, and Western, Hughes well understood the value of the airplane as the most popular method of transporting tourists and gamblers to Las Vegas. Having sold ownership of TWA for $560 million in 1966, Hughes bought the Air West merger for $94 million, assuming $40 million of the company's debt.[26] After managerial restructuring and replacement of DC-9-10 jets seating 75 passengers with newer DC-9-30 jets seating 103 passengers, in 1974, the airline finally made a profit of $7.9 million.[27] Hughes Air West did exceedingly well as a competitor, especially in the southwestern market. The airline reported monthly passenger hauls of 254,700 passengers, a 65–75 percent passenger load factor, making it the leading carrier in the short-haul market.[28] But in the mid-1970s, the quality of passenger service declined as the airline received numerous complaints from customers about tardiness, unfriendly customer service, and too few flights (such as no morning flight from Las Vegas to Reno). In fact, an editorial in the Las Vegas Review-Journal called for more airline competition because it claimed Hughes Air West had a monopoly on the Las Vegas–to–Reno route and was not fulfilling its promise to Nevadans that it would offer five daily flights between the two cities, since it scheduled only four. Residents in Reno and Las Vegas complained to their city commissioners, who then asked the

Nevada Public Service Commission to step in, seeking a resolution from state legislators mandating that the airline improve the quality of its service. The airline responded to the complaints by claiming that it was waiting for Civil Aeronautics Board approval of the airline's application for authorization to fly from Las Vegas to Seattle via Reno and Portland.[29]

The CAB approved the application on condition that Hughes Air West adjust its schedule to include a morning flight. Western Airlines also added two morning flights to Reno to become competitive with Hughes Air West. But the complaints did not discourage Hughes, ever the aviation business-man, who dreamed of making Las Vegas an aviation center and a model metropolis. His plan involved converting McCarran Airport into a supersonic transportation facility that could accommodate the Concorde, a jet capable of carrying 200 passengers from New York to Paris at a speed of 1,350 miles per hour in a little more than three hours. County commissioner Bill Briare, McCarran Airport manager Erle Taylor, and Las Vegas Chamber of Com-merce president Gaylord Prather responded with "cautious optimism that Las Vegas might become the site of a supersonic transport air terminal serv-ing the entire southwestern United States."[30] Taylor expressed his excitement about Hughes's endorsement that McCarran Airport would need further expansion, including runway extensions and more buildings to accommo-date "jumbo airliners and the supersonic transport."[31] County commissioner Briare lauded Hughes for his forward thinking about the future of commer-cial aviation in Las Vegas: "This exciting suggestion by the Hughes people confirms our [county commission's] thinking that the future of Las Vegas lies in the airways. We have the potential of being the world's largest air center."[32] Las Vegas Chamber of Commerce president Prather echoed the sentiments of Briare and Taylor: "We [the Chamber of Commerce] are supporting expan-sion of the airport for jumbo jets, but believe the airport should stay close to the community and especially close to the tourist-oriented community of Las Vegas."[33]

Another part of Hughes's plan was to bring airplane manufacturing giant Boeing to Las Vegas. Hughes owned 40,000 acres of land around McCarran Airport, which included much of the Strip, and he offered Boeing 20,000 acres upon which to build an airplane manufacturing plant. According to Las Vegas historian Eugene Moehring, Boeing considered moving to south-ern Nevada because of its less pro-union environment, warm weather, and friendly tax structure for businesses. The deal fell through, however, suppos-edly because of months of inaction and Boeing's fear of relocating its workers to a city where they could cash their paychecks at the casinos.[34] But Boeing must have been aware of the support of organized-crime figures for labor unions, which was a major deterrent. Additionally, the giant airplane manufacturer must have known about the troubled history between Hughes and the Las Vegas City Council over property acquisition.

With Hughes buying most of the casinos on the Strip and land around McCarran Airport, the Las Vegas City Council blocked him from acquiring any more property in Las Vegas for fear of his taking ownership and control of the city. The city council accused him of breaking antitrust laws.[35] As a result, Hughes was unable to realize his hopes of turning McCarran Airport into a supersonic airport for the Concorde. When Hughes died in 1976, his airline merged with Republic Airlines, a Minneapolis-based regional air carrier that less than a decade later became the tenth-largest U.S. airline, serving more cities, including Las Vegas.[36] It was not long, however, before Republic and other airlines began replacing their jets with newer ones.

Like their predecessors the propeller-driven Douglas DC-6 and the Lockheed Constellation, the popular Boeing 707 and the Douglas DC-8 became outmoded as the airline industry continued to expand at a prolific rate. In the mid- to late 1960s, the Boeing 727, 737, the Douglas DC-9, and the wide-bodied Boeing 747, Douglas DC-10, and Lockheed TriStar L-1011 became the foundation for modern passenger jet travel. Able to carry even more passengers, have more-fuel-efficient engines, and fly even greater distances without refueling, this second generation of passenger jets once again revolutionized the commercial air travel industry.

The Boeing 737, a twin-engine jet with a seating capacity of 126 passengers and a fuel range allowing it to fly nonstop from Seattle to Las Vegas, became a favorite of air travelers because of its comfort, speed, and ability to land at smaller airports. The jet's ability to fly short and medium distances without refueling enabled airlines to offer service to more cities, better schedules (flight frequency), and lower fares, because this jet was not as expensive to operate as its larger predecessor, the Boeing 707. The addition of newer, smaller jets and more flights intensified competition in the Las Vegas market as airlines placed multiple orders for the 737 and its competitor, the Douglas DC-9, so they could offer flights to Las Vegas from smaller cities in Washington, Oregon, California, and Arizona.

Another jet that contributed to the revolution in Las Vegas air travel was the Douglas DC-10, a wide-bodied jet with seating for 290 passengers and the fuel range to fly nonstop from Honolulu. The advent of this jumbo jet in Las

Vegas marked the beginning of yet another period of rapid advancement in commercial air travel as it and other wide-bodied jets such as the Lockheed L-1011 and the Boeing 747 enabled airlines to transport people from London, Paris, and Frankfurt to Las Vegas in little more than half a day. These aircraft also elevated Las Vegas to the level of world-class tourist cities such as San Francisco, Los Angeles, Paris, and Tokyo. Of course, the size and weight of these jets meant that airports such as McCarran had to extend runways more than two miles in total length and renovate gates with jetways to enable passengers to safely and comfortably enplane and deplane. McCarran Airport officials would have to find additional funds for airport expansion.

Jetports, like money, do not grow on trees. In fact, they require dollars. During the 1960s and 1970s, the skyrocketing demand for air travel and the introduction of jets to airline fleets augmented air traffic and terminal congestion to the point that airport officials had to accelerate expensive expansion plans. Runways had to be lengthened and reinforced with better and more durable concrete, taxiways required widening and extending, aprons needed to be built, and better runway lighting had to be installed for jets to operate safely at night and to land in bad weather. Like McCarran, airports in Los Angeles, San Diego, and across the nation needed better air traffic control centers and airport towers, with proper equipment to handle the increased traffic, improved navigation equipment for airplane instrument approaches, and more ticket counter space, baggage carousels, and gates. To cover the cost, airlines and local governments once again turned to Washington.

Federal aid for airport expansion was usually slow in coming, for several reasons: political bickering among Democrats and Republicans in Washington, D.C., priority placed on increased automobile travel and the need for highway construction, and, always, budgetary concerns. Airport officials typically had to plan two to three years ahead for growth needs and search for state and local funding. Even after Congress passed the Federal Airport Act in 1946, which promised $500 million over seven years for new airport construction, expansion, and improvement of the nation's commercial airports, in reality each year's received allocation was less than what President Harry S. Truman requested because Congress claimed the allocations would add to the national deficit.[37] In the end, however, the government–airline industry partnership endured and federal funding continued.

After President Truman created the Air Policy Commission to conduct a comprehensive review of the nation's air travel system, Congress approved a recommended $40 million for continued government subsidization of the airlines, modernization of the nation's airways, installation of weather navigation systems, and research and development programs for better aviation technology. In 1953, under the Federal Aid Airport Program, Congress appropriated $13 million for airport expansion and other aviation facilities improvements. Because of increased air travel demand and rapid growth of the airline industry, in 1954 the appropriation increased to $30 million and in 1959 to $58 million.[38]

The Eisenhower administration (1953–1961) ordered a task force to conduct a comprehensive study on the state of the commercial airline industry and the nation's airports. The findings clearly showed insufficient funding to airports for upgrading their facilities to meet the needs of the airlines and air travelers. Yet the budget-conscious Republican administration felt no sense of urgency, rather believing that the previous allocations were sufficient. Instead, Eisenhower prioritized funding to improve the nation's highways and roads under the Federal Highway Act of 1956.[39] While this piece of legislation was an enormous boon for the oil, automobile, construction, and trucking industries and advanced highway safety, it overlooked the explosive growth of air travel, which by the late 1950s had surpassed train travel and closely rivaled automobile travel. After Eisenhower left office, funding for commercial air travel during the Kennedy and Johnson administrations (1961–1969) was substantially increased, largely because of the steady growth in passenger volume and the number of aircraft in service.

In a letter to the Senate and the House of Representatives, President Kennedy wrote: "Air Commerce since the enactment of the Federal Airport Act of 1946 has grown so rapidly that many existing airport facilities are both overburdened and underequipped. The increase in speed, weight, and capacity of jet age aircraft has already antiquated existing airports and threatens to outmode many more."[40] From 1963 to 1967, the number of annual commercial flights increased from 87,267 to 116,796, and passenger volume, which barely exceeded 126 million prior to 1963, nearly doubled in that year alone. In response, the Kennedy administration in conjunction with Congress increased the allocation to airports to $75 million a year. President Lyndon Johnson increased it again, to $200 million a year. In May 1970 Congress passed the Airport and Airway Development Act, which provided even greater funds for airports: $250 million for facilities and equipment and $150 million for airport construction projects.[41] Airport officials essentially looked at airport improvement design to address passenger conveniences, airline efficiency, economy in construction, and operational safety. McCarran Airport in Las Vegas was a candidate for airport improvement funding.

In 1960, after Las Vegas voters approved the $5 million bond, airport director Gordon Miles and his staff immediately began the expansion of McCarran Airport. The plan was to extend the airport eastward across neighboring desert flats to provide additional necessary space for both passenger jets and charter planes. Contractors lengthened runways, widened taxiways, and enlarged the terminal, but with 99 flights per day and more than one million passengers moving through the terminal, the airport still lacked sufficient space.

In 1961, with the help of a federal grant of $943,121 procured by Nevada senators Alan Bible and Howard Cannon, construction of a new jetport named McCarran Airport began at a different location, today's Paradise Road and Russell Road.[42] Completed in 1963, the jetport consisted of a 262,000-square-foot clamshell-shaped three-level terminal with airline ticket counters, baggage carousels, the Flight Deck Restaurant, the Omni Bar, shops that annually brought in more than $34 million, terminal gates, two runways (one 10,200 feet long and the other 8,900 feet long), taxiways, a 239,610-square-yard apron for commercial airline use only, and parking spaces for automobiles.[43]

The new McCarran jetport opened on March 15, 1963. In its first year the facility handled more than 1.5 million passengers and averaged 128 flights a day.[44] Seven airlines served McCarran: Pacific Airlines, Delta, American, and the original four—Bonanza, United, TWA, and Western. A spokesman for Lembke Construction Company of Nevada publicly proclaimed: "There are few airports in the country that can compare in facilities and design to the McCarran Field Terminal."[45] The *Las Vegas Review-Journal* praised the airport as the embodiment of "determination and vision when the prospect of air transportation had become an integral part of the development of Las Vegas and the new McCarran Airport Terminal."[46] The building of this new airport was significant because it confirmed what had been happening since the beginning of commercial aviation in Las Vegas: the city was becoming increasingly dependent on commercial airlines to deliver tourists and business travelers, and the airlines themselves were becoming a critical and growing part of the city. In a letter to McCarran Airport director Gordon Miles, Senator Bible congratulated him on the new airport, saying, "Please accept my congratulations for one of America's most modern airports. The completion of this facility really puts Nevada into the jet age, and I predict that the tremendous passenger volume will soar to even greater heights in the foreseeable future. This airport is a living testimonial to harmonious and productive cooperation between the federal and local governments."[47] Las Vegas finally had a large enough airport to handle more than a million passengers and more than double the flights of 1960.

In October 1967 the number of passengers rose to 683,773, setting a record for the largest monthly passenger volume in airport history.[48] The new jetport needed much more space and was operating $1 million in the red because of higher overhead costs, which included maintenance and upkeep, and more airport staff. Airport manager Erle Taylor, who replaced Gordon Miles in 1966, said it would take the airport two years to get out of debt because of the great increase in tourism and air travel that made it difficult for the airport to keep up. He and his staff immediately moved forward with plans for further expansion: doubling the size of the terminals, lengthening runways, widening taxiways, and adding thirty-six more gates.[49] The construction got under way in 1968.

The expansion project, completed on September 6, 1974, carried with it a hefty price tag of $30 million. This time the county commissioners found a new source of funding to avoid antagonizing local residents with more bond issues every time the airport needed additional facilities. Bonds were sold to businesses and wealthy city residents and cost the taxpayers nothing. The airport was finally able to pay its own expenses because it made a tremendous profit from increasing landing fees, leasing the gates, ticket counters, and baggage carousels to commercial airlines, and leasing terminal space to concessions (slot machines monthly brought in $100,000 in revenue, as did food courts and shops), in addition to the sale of these bonds.[50] McCarran Airport revenue was essential because the metropolitan area's population base of 125,787 residents in 1970 made it difficult for the county to rely on taxpayers as the primary source of funding for airport expansion.[51] The airport had to become self-sustaining, and it did. But the newly completed expansion project was inadequate, and in fact symbolized a problem for Las Vegas. A constant need for airport expansion, a growing urban population, and skyrocketing passenger volume presented city and airport officials with the challenge of keeping up. Sun and fun, gambling, entertainment, conventions, and jobs kept the masses coming to Las Vegas, which in turn required more flights, a larger airport, and bigger casino-resort hotels.

By 1973 the passenger volume reached 5 million travelers, too many for the $30 million expansion project. By 1976, the airport was struggling to handle 317 daily flight arrivals and an annual passenger volume of 5,944,433, with projections of 10 million in 1980.[52] Plans that had been drawn up by airport contractors Landrum and Brown for the next two decades had to be changed. The contractors urged the airport to immediately purchase 3,000 more acres of land for further runway extension, more taxiways, a strengthened apron for heavy jets, a new runway in 1990, and sixty-nine additional gates by 1995. It also recommended that the old airport acquire more property for construction of a new terminal, runways, and taxiways for general aviation and charter operators. The projected price was $276,575,700.[53]

In 1976 airport director Erle Taylor hired TRA Airport Consulting to get a second bid (it was common for airports to solicit bids from multiple contractors to find the best offer). In its 1979 executive summary, TRA recommended construction of a third runway at the new airport, terminal expansion to include three satellites, and a people mover system. Planners for TRA and Landrum and Brown, clearly recognizing the need for immediate expansion, reported: "The terminal building is now burdened with more passengers and airplanes that it can comfortably accommodate. . . . Every part of the facility is overcrowded, from ticketing and baggage areas to coffee shops and restrooms." It predicted that by 1995 "passenger loads would exceed 30 million and the number of commercial aircraft seeking to use the airfield would more than double."[54] TRA won the contract and began construction in 1980. But the overarching question was how to fund the expansion.

To help finance the project, the Federal Aviation Administration provided $106,253,900 in funding through the Airport Development Aid Program, leaving airport officials to come up with $170,321,800, which they did through bond sales, airline takeoff and landing fees, rent for ticket counter space and concourse gates, concession fees, and slot machine revenue.[55]

In the 1960s and 1970s, as major airlines United, Western, Delta, TWA, and smaller regional and charter airlines delivered millions of worldwide passengers to Las Vegas, they not only required McCarran International Airport to expand, but also prompted the casino-resort industry to build larger and more elegant properties. With the airline industry booming, casino executives, in cooperation with the Las Vegas Chamber of Commerce, the Las Vegas Convention and Visitors Authority (LVCVA), and McCarran International Airport, sought ways to attract as many air travelers as possible. They did this by building high-rise, super-luxurious resorts. The 700-room Caesars Palace was a first-class resort completed in 1966 by Cabana Motel chain owner Jay Sarno, an award-winning designer, builder, and hotelier.

With approval from Teamsters Union president Jimmy Hoffa and organized-crime member Murray Humphreys's front man Allen Dorfman, Sarno
received $20 million from the Teamsters Union Pension Fund to develop
the property, the most money ever spent on a resort. In an attempt to quash
the deal, the FBI leaked a wiretap report to Sandy Smith, a reporter for the
Chicago Tribune, fingering Sarno as a front man for the Chicago Mafia.[56]
While the negative publicity angered Mafia bosses, the public still felt no
qualms over gambling, shopping, and staying at the European-style resort.
With its Ancient Rome theme, including fountains and statues, and an 800-
seat Circus Maximus patterned after the Coliseum, Caesars was the place
in town for performances by top entertainers, among them Frank Sinatra,
Ella Fitzgerald, Paul Anka, and Tony Bennett. More than 20,000 people daily
walked through the property's doors. They gambled, dined at five-star restaurants and buffets, shopped, and sunbathed by the resort's Olympic-size
and lavishly decorated swimming pools.

Sarno would be outdone by Kirk Kerkorian, a former crop duster, cargo
pilot, and charter airline owner from Southern California who also wanted to
establish himself in Las Vegas as a casino-resort magnate. In 1969 Kerkorian
built the largest casino-resort in Las Vegas's history, the $60 million Inter-
national Hotel, a towering property with 1,600 rooms and a 30,000-square-
foot casino, symbolizing a new era in the casino-resort industry.[57] One of the
largest hotels in the world, it attracted top entertainers to Las Vegas, among
them Barbra Streisand, Sammy Davis Jr., Dean Martin, Dom DeLuise, Joey
Bishop, and Johnny Carson. The stars typically commissioned $100,000 a
week and filled auditoriums with hotel guests and local residents nightly.
Three years later, Kerkorian would outdo the International by building the
$120 million, 2,089-room MGM Grand, a massive property based on the 1932
Hollywood film *Grand Hotel,* where five guests who had never before met
spent two days interacting in Berlin's plush Grand Hotel. The MGM's restaurants were run by world-class chefs, and the property housed an enormous casino, two showrooms—one for the entertainers and the other for
production shows—Olympic-size swimming pools, and health spas. With
the casino-resorts responding to the growing air travel and tourism industries by expanding their properties or building larger, newer ones, the symbiotic relationship between the airlines, the airport, and the casino-resorts
strengthened, with a forecast of additional growth.

According to Paul Titus, director of marketing, advertising, and tourism
at the Las Vegas Convention and Visitors Authority, future outlook plans for

continued hotel room expansion called for 49,000 total rooms by 1980 and 64,000 by 1985.[58] But the low-rise resort motels built in the 1940s by Griffith, Moore, Siegel, and other pioneering hoteliers, which were enormously popular in their day, made it possible for Sarno, Kerkorian, and other high-rise resort magnates to build their massive properties and to attract the millions of guests who visited their properties. Sarno and Kerkorian built upon the concept of the casino-resort in the southern Nevada desert by taking the original idea and expanding on it.

Construction of these new resorts also created jobs. The casinos needed gaming dealers, bartenders, cocktail waitresses, hotel registration staff, managers, and maintenance personnel, which kept unemployment low. Keith Schwer, director of the University of Nevada, Las Vegas Center for Business and Economic Research, has explained that the city's circle of growth "starts with the building of new resorts, which results in larger visitor volumes, which results in increased gaming revenue, which results in more employment, which results in more population, which results in more home construction, and more personal income."[59]

Low taxation on businesses and a favorable year-round climate also prompted businesses from other cities to relocate to Las Vegas. A 1961 article in *Holiday* magazine proclaimed: "The city extols its broad streets, ranch-style homes, first-rate schools, eighty-one church groups, four hospitals, and no state income tax. Most Las Vegans felt satisfied with their city and its economy. If outsiders like U.S. senators did not agree, let them stay away from this amusing, colorful, and interesting town."[60]

In 1978 Las Vegas was no longer a young city but had become a maturing city, with a population nearing 165,000, churches, schools (including the city's first university, the University of Nevada, Las Vegas, which opened in 1957), and parks.[61] With the explosive increase in air travel to Las Vegas, a larger and more cosmopolitan airport, and expanding casino resorts, the city stood to benefit from public works projects such as the construction of Bond Road (today Tropicana Avenue, an eight-lane major route connecting the airport with downtown), which enabled tourists, business travelers, and conventioneers arriving at McCarran International Airport to speed to the Las Vegas Strip in less than ten minutes. This new road prompted airport director Erle Taylor to include $900,000 in his budget for upgrading roadway systems.[62] All of this growth underscored the importance of commercial air travel and its effect on cities, including Las Vegas.

Western historian Earl Pomeroy confirmed that "air service ultimately justified much of the confidence of its [Las Vegas's] advocates, transforming cities and their tributary territory at least as much as ship and railroad had done earlier. Within two decades, between the 1950s and the 1970s, Las Vegas became the fastest-growing metropolitan area in the mountain states region after patrons of its casinos began arriving by air."[63]

By 1976 Convention and Visitors Authority statistics showed that Las Vegas had become the number one tourist destination in the country, with 9.8 million visitors, a 6.8 percent increase from 1975 and a 44 percent increase from 1970.[64] Four million of these visitors arrived by plane.[65] The city's tourist increase mirrored the larger national trend in air travel. Between 1955 and 1978, the number of airline travelers in the United States rose from 41 million to 275 million.[66] The postwar increase in population, in affluent Americans, and in a well-employed working class all contributed to staggering tourist growth that was greater than that of any other industry in the nation. The airlines and travel agents took advantage of a growing consumerism that focused on travel by using massive promotions of economy fares and package vacations.

Until this time, airline passengers had usually been leisure-class travelers who could afford long, expensive trips and businessmen who chose air travel for its speed and became its most frequent fliers. After World War II, modern mass tourism—middle- and working-class fliers—encouraged the airline industry to democratize air travel by introducing coach service with economy fares and package deals. Pan Am's president, Juan Trippe, called the introduction of coach-class service the third major milestone in aviation history; Lindbergh's famous 1927 flight from New York to Paris, the first; and the advent of the jetliner, the second.[67] When the smaller, non-scheduled airlines began specializing in fast, efficient, total coach service, the big four airlines— United, TWA, Pan Am, and American—jumped on the bandwagon and set up first class, business class, and coach class.

As air travel grew, tourism grew. Travelers had to have a place to stay, which prompted the airlines to persuade the hotel industry to get involved, building hotels wherever there were airline passengers. By the 1960s "there were Hiltons, Hyatts, and Sheratons to house deplaning Americans almost everywhere."[68] The advent of credit cards further accelerated air travel and hotel stays. Pan Am adopted the slogan "Fly now and pay later," and attracted thousands of domestic and international travelers. Travel agents picked up on the credit policy, and booked their customers a complete travel agenda with airline tickets, transportation service, and hotel service, all on the credit plan.[69]

As a result of the introduction of coach-class travel, the ability to fly using a credit card, and the use of jets, the nature of air travel changed. The focus in prewar days had been on the excitement and prestige of flying. The selling point was the airplane. But as planes became larger, flew faster and higher, and were crowded with coach-fare travelers, the focus of the trip became the destination. Las Vegas capitalized on this development through larger casinos, more luxurious and comfortable hotel rooms, premier entertainment, top recreation facilities, nicely manicured golf courses, and excellent customer service. With the partnership of jetliners, the jetport, the Las Vegas Convention and Visitors Authority, the Las Vegas Chamber of Commerce, and government funding, Las Vegas became an ideal model for selling the destination, a winning technique for making the passenger volume mushroom. Airlines touted Las Vegas as the resort city in the desert.

In 1960 Western Airlines transported 21,501 passengers to Las Vegas, TWA 18,103, and United 11,370. A decade later, those numbers had increased more than tenfold: Western Airlines transported more than 231,000 passengers monthly, Hughes Air West 224,000, United 151,000, and TWA 141,000.[70] With such a significant increase in passenger volume, the Flamingo Hotel opened a "flight wing" to help guests with reservations and accommodations on Hughes Air West, TWA, United, and Western. The MGM Grand and the Riviera opened Delta Airlines ticket offices where guests could purchase one-way travel to Atlanta on the TriStar L-1011 for $154 in first class or $123 in coach. Guests also could purchase one-way travel to Charlotte via Atlanta on the TriStar L-1011 for $170 in first class or $136 in coach.[71]

In 1970, for a modern desert city with a metropolitan population of 273,000, more than four million air travelers annually arriving at McCarran Airport, and a booming tourism industry, Las Vegas's future looked endlessly bright. The passenger volume and airport growth in Las Vegas were phenomenal compared to that of Phoenix, another southwestern desert city, with a population of 470,000 and a passenger volume of 2.9 million travelers, or that of San Diego, with a population of 697,000 and a passenger volume of 3.3 million. But problems with government regulation of the airline industry and the airlines themselves led to a major shakeup that strongly affected the nation, including Las Vegas.

A Western Air Express Douglas M-2 used for transporting mail is being refueled at Rockwell field before it departs for Los Angeles. Courtesy of Howard W. Cannon Aviation Museum.

"Wild Bill" Morgan hands Western Air Express pilot Jimmie James a bag of mail at Rockwell Field on the inaugural airmail flight of the CAM-4 route from Salt Lake City to Los Angeles on April 17, 1926. Courtesy of Howard W. Cannon Aviation Museum.

A Hacienda Airlines Lockheed Constellation is parked at McCarran Airport in 1961. It was one of eight airplanes used for junket flights to Las Vegas. Courtesy of Howard W. Cannon Aviation Museum.

A Bonanza Airlines DC-3 gives passengers an aerial tour of the Hoover Dam as part of a promotional sightseeing package. Courtesy of Howard W. Cannon Aviation Museum.

FACING PAGE:

Top: An aerial view of the "C" gates at McCarran International Airport in 1998 before it became entirely occupied by Southwest Airlines. The mega-resorts are in the background. Courtesy of Howard W. Cannon Aviation Museum.

Bottom: An aerial view of McCarran International Airport in the 1970s with the Dunes Hotel and Resort in the foreground. Courtesy of Howard W. Cannon Aviation Museum.

CHAPTER FOUR

Airline Deregulation and the Mega-Resorts

*C*ongressional passage of the Airline Deregulation Act of 1978 could not have come at a better time for Las Vegas. Struggling to shed its reputation as a bastion of gambling, booze, sex, drugs, and organized crime, Las Vegas set out to seriously re-create its image, representing the new Las Vegas as a modern metropolis resembling other well-known cities in the nation and the world. Construction of exquisite high-rise casino-resorts run by Wall Street corporations instead of by Mafia bosses, an ambitious $30 million McCarran International Airport expansion plan, and seventeen airlines annually bringing in seven million passengers offered the city an opportunity to extricate itself from its hedonistic past. Such important changes would profoundly affect the existing symbiotic relationships among air travel, airport, and destination. The airlines needed to increase passenger flights from both national and international cities of origin. McCarran had to install longer runways for larger aircraft and build more modern terminals housing a variety of restaurants, lounges, and shops to accommodate huge numbers of travelers. Sparing no expense, corporate businesses intent on attracting world travelers had to design and build the most luxurious of mega-resorts with no fewer than 3,000 hotel rooms and modern state-of-the-art gaming tables and slot machines.

By 1985 the number of airlines serving Las Vegas had increased from seventeen to twenty-one, a remarkable jump for a high-volume, low-yield leisure market that did not have the same profitability as the high-volume, high-yield business markets of Los Angeles, San Francisco, Chicago, and New York, which were dominated by the major airlines.[1] While these cities attracted predominantly business and international travelers who were willing to pay higher fares, Las Vegas was just the opposite—it lured leisure travelers by offering bargain-basement fares from airlines like Southwest, America West, and National. Casino-resorts such as the Landmark, the MGM

Grand, and Caesars Palace offered discounted room rates to attract more customers, and that, along with the cheap airfares, was a winning combination for middle- and lower-income Americans. Duane Busch, TWA executive station manager in Las Vegas, confirmed this when he commented: "Deregulation afforded middle- and lower-income people the opportunity to travel at an affordable rate."[2] Southwest offered one-way fares from Las Vegas to Los Angeles and other California destinations for $29, a deal that was extremely difficult for United, Delta, and other major airlines to match.[3] America West and National followed Southwest's lead by creating their own niches in national markets, including the Las Vegas market, through cheap "red-eye" flights and low-fare transcontinental flights from Las Vegas to East Coast cities. Airlines like Southwest, America West, and National thrived on the business model of low fares, multiple flights, and excellent customer service, and cities like Phoenix, Las Vegas, and San Diego profited immensely from the resulting increases in the numbers of business and leisure travelers.

Though deregulation brought great benefits to low-fare carriers and large cities, it also had its problems. Appearing before the Subcommittee on Aviation of the U.S. House of Representatives Committee on Transportation and Infrastructure, Joseph Leonard, CEO of AirTran, testified that smaller airlines such as his could not compete in certain markets—Minneapolis, Chicago, Atlanta, and Dallas among them—because of the dominance of the major airlines at hub airports.[4] At a hearing of the Senate Committee on Commerce, Science, and Transportation, he and other regional airline executives expressed their concern about trying to compete in an environment of "predatory behavior where one airline accounts for more than 50% of the traffic."[5] This became problematic for second- and third-tier cities where residents had to drive to larger airports to catch their flights because the hub-and-spoke system was inconvenient and expensive. Passengers could not fly directly from one second- or third-tier city to another. They had to connect through a hub airport, which was time-consuming and unaffordable. The major airlines made substantial profits through this hub-and-spoke system because connecting flights ensured larger passenger loads. They opposed any policy changes that threatened the existing system, including deregulation. But during the Carter and Reagan administrations, the government viewed deregulation slightly differently.

According to the U.S. General Accounting Office, if Congress had passed legislation deregulating the airline industry a decade earlier, "airlines could have operated at a far lower cost, annually saving air travelers $1.4–$1.8 billion."[6] When the Civil Aeronautics Board controlled fares, it was reluctant to lower them too much because the airlines and the government each needed to make a profit. The high operating costs of passenger jets, increased wage demands by airline employees, and airport expansion costs required the CAB to keep fares at a high level as well. But high fares also had the effect of slowing demand for air travel. The General Accounting Office reported that during regulation the CAB kept fares 22–52 percent higher than they would have been under deregulation.[7] If the board had lowered fares, more people would have chosen to fly, and the airlines and government would have experienced greater profit. Also, according to transcripts of an October 1999 testimony before the House of Representatives Committee on Transportation and Infrastructure, "during the past twenty years, deregulation and competition lowered fares by more than 40%. This was especially true when a low-cost carrier entered the market. Fares dropped by 50%. Three times as many people fly now as they did before deregulation."[8] Secretary of Transportation Federico Peña stated in 1995 that the airline industry saved $6.3 billion as a result of low-cost competition.[9] A 1995 Brookings Institution study stated that lower airfares saved the traveling public $12.4 billion per year.[10] Hence it is no surprise that deregulation facilitated substantial passenger volume growth in most markets.

According to other government records, after deregulation was imposed, regional and commuter airlines passenger volume grew by 20 percent, departures at major hubs increased by 15.7 percent, medium-airport growth was up by 22.5 percent, and small-airport growth increased by 12.4 percent.[11] But Las Vegas stood to benefit the most from airline deregulation because it expanded the city's primary sources of revenue: tourism and gambling. And airlines such as Southwest, America West, and National took advantage of it.

Susan Davis, Las Vegas marketing representative for Southwest Airlines, emphasized the airline's financial success and growth based on its philosophy of "the three Fs: fun, fares, and frequency." The airline prided itself on friendly customer service, offering low fares and on-time flights to more than one hundred destinations nationwide. It became a formidable contender in the Las Vegas market, in 1996 transporting 22.7 percent of the 30,459,965 passengers who came to McCarran International Airport. Because of its reputation, reliability, and affordability, from 1997 to 2001, Southwest led all other airlines in passenger transportation volume, bringing more than 30 percent of the travelers to Las Vegas.[12]

Southwest Airlines was founded in 1971 by an astute and aggressive businessman who had a penchant for smoking packs of Camels, drank Wild Turkey whiskey, and transported himself to and from work on a Harley-Davidson motorcycle. CEO Herb Kelleher sought to dominate the national airline markets, and he did just that. Beginning with three Boeing 737s, offering low fares, and instructing flight attendants to provide excellent in-flight service, the airline enjoyed remarkable success as one of the most popular interstate regional carriers. Originally the airline offered service within the state of Texas, where it crafted its business model. Within two years, however, it sought to expand service to other cities in the Southwest that had underserved airports. Kelleher's airline soared because of simple marketing strategies that were specially tailored to cities, like Las Vegas, that were ready to accommodate a different clientele than in years past. Southwest's planes offered only one class of service catering to all customers.

With some of the best low fares in the market, two-for-the-price-of-one deals under the "Friends Fly Free" program, and bonus rewards for the number of trips flown, Southwest quickly developed a large working-class clientele. With two hundred daily arrivals and departures at McCarran International Airport, Southwest, with a primary hub in Phoenix, opened a second hub in Las Vegas, making the Nevada resort city the airline's top market. The airline rapidly became the favorite of air travelers. Southwest's Las Vegas marketing representative, Susan Davis, emphasized that the airline "tried to target 'young-minded' travelers, but catered to all passengers. . . . So there really was no specific focus on any type of passenger." She added that the airline "also strategically focused on a 'short-haul' market where the average flight did not exceed a five-hundred-mile radius or a flight time of more than two hours."[13]

To improve its service, the airline created many methods for quick turnaround, such as deplaning and enplaning passengers in as little as fifteen minutes by not assigning seats, a strategy that effectively avoided costly delays at the gate. By the late 1990s, Southwest had become so popular among tourists and gamblers that it was the sole tenant of McCarran's Concourse C. According to Ginger Hardage, vice president of public relations, the airline offered nonstop flights to twenty-seven destinations, including New Orleans, Nashville, San Antonio, Tulsa, and Omaha.[14] Passengers thus had more choices and fares that were competitive with those of Delta, one of Southwest's greatest rivals serving the southern United States. Low fares, reasonable hotel rates, affordable entertainment, inexpensive recreation, and gambling created an ideal atmosphere for Southwest, McCarran International Airport, and the tourism and gambling industries to continue growing together.

In contrast to Southwest Airlines, America West Airlines, a strong competitor in the Las Vegas market, focused on the business traveler. Headquartered in Tempe, Arizona, and flying Boeing 737s, 757s, and Airbus A-319s and A-320s, in the Southwest and other regions of the country, America West took a different approach to air travel. One of the airline's marketing managers, Jennifer Myers, explained: "Because the airline catered to the business traveler, it provided more flights in certain markets that proved to be more profitable."[15] To accomplish this, America West scheduled a majority of its flights to depart from Los Angeles, Phoenix, Las Vegas, and San Francisco so business travelers could easily make connecting flights to eastern destinations. Myers said, "The airline had a complex system, more so than passengers just flying to Las Vegas to stay there. . . . Las Vegas was primarily a connecting airport for a majority of America West's older passengers."[16]

The airline also created a niche by scheduling many of its flights in the evening and late at night ("red-eye" flights) because those times for travel proved to be the most in demand and the most profitable for business and leisure travelers wanting to arrive on the East Coast early in the morning of the next day. Since no other airline at McCarran International Airport featured an entire bank of late-night flights, America West executives seized the opportunity to increase business and profits by offering low fares for those flights. Most people travel during the day and pay higher fares, but those hunting for cheaper fares were amenable to flying late at night.

According to Myers, another America West strategy was to observe a geographic region to identify which airline was dominant there and what its strategy was. America West would then move in and offer competitive fares and provide amenities that the other carriers did not provide in order to capture the lion's share of the market. Among the amenities were first-class or business-class sections with wider and more comfortable seats. Passengers enjoyed meals and sipped their beverages from real glasses rather than from plastic cups. The airline also offered in-flight movies and multiple music stations with headphones.[17] This marketing strategy, in addition to the low fares, enabled America West to compete in the Southwest region, including in the profitable Las Vegas market, because that was what the new Las Vegas mandated: cheap and available flights, discounted hotel rooms, affordable entertainment, and plenty of amenities for middle- and lower-income tourists.

Michael Conway, the CEO of National Airlines, Las Vegas's "hometown airline," adopted a philosophy similar to that of America West: catering to the business traveler, leisure tourist, and Las Vegas resident. By offering inexpensive transcontinental flights from Las Vegas to eastern destinations like Philadelphia, Chicago, and New York, Conway believed, he could attract more business travelers and tourists than his competitors did. For instance, in 1997 passengers could fly round-trip from Las Vegas to Miami for $238.[18] Since Las Vegas was such a popular destination for air travelers and a city that attracted many businesses, Conway felt it was the ideal base for his airline. He contended that "for a true hub-and-spoke market to be successful, the hub of the operation must be a strong destination in and of itself."[19] Also, by using one type of aircraft, the Boeing 757, he kept the airline's maintenance and pilot-training costs to a minimum.

In its first year of business, National Airlines was successful, but during its second year the airline went into the red, for three reasons. First, the rising cost of fuel consumed much of the airline's capital, accounting for more than 40 percent of its operating expenses.[20] Like other airlines, National felt the pain of high fuel prices dating back to the OPEC crisis in 1973, when a domestic oil shortage and an increased demand for Middle Eastern oil caused prices to skyrocket. Subsequent spikes in oil prices in 1979, 1990, and 1999 also caused airlines to raise their fares.[21] From 1988 to 1992, the airlines collectively had lost more than $12 billion, and the sharp increases in oil prices prompted President Clinton to hold an emergency meeting with his Cabinet and oil company executives to search for desperately needed solutions, but none were found. Clinton blamed it on the government's "failure to create an economic climate necessary for this leading-edge industry [commercial aviation] to thrive at home and in an increasingly global economy."[22] But as long as fuel prices remained high and the airlines kept losing money, they became more dependent on the federal government for subsidization in the form of loans to help keep them afloat—which was actually nothing new. Similar conditions had existed since the airline industry's inception.

A second reason for National's economic strife was its route system, which included flights from Las Vegas to San Francisco and Los Angeles, short-haul routes that were not economically sensible for gas-guzzling Boeing 757s which were passenger planes designed for long-haul transcontinental flights. The airline had placed orders for 737s for the short-haul flights, but with massive debt and insufficient capital from financial backers, including Harrah's and the Rio casino-resorts, National officials had to cancel the orders and file for bankruptcy in 2000. Shortly thereafter, the airline went out of business.

A third and final problem for National was the intense pressure in the form of special package deals between the major airlines and other casino-resorts on the Strip that viewed Harrah's and the Rio's support of an airline as a threat. As Las Vegas historian Hal Rothman observed, "The casinos could not afford to antagonize the major airlines. They depended on all of the airlines to bring them passengers, and if one of the big four carriers perceived the casinos as competition, the airlines could confidently move their seats to more lucrative routes."[23] With the new competition that developed when the airline industry was deregulated, some airlines were forced to reduce their number of flights to Las Vegas, or in TWA's case, to completely pull out of the Las Vegas market. Rothman also noted that the airlines were cutting back on the number of flights and seats to Las Vegas because other markets were more profitable: "The combination of price-sensitive vacation travelers and the discount packages that defined the local market meant that on a per seat basis when demand almost exceeded supply, business travelers between Chicago and Los Angeles offered far higher profit per traveler. The major airlines cut their flights to Las Vegas to maximize profit from market conditions."[24] Hence, when National Airlines CEO Conway tried to carve out a new niche by offering cheap transcontinental flights, his airline could not remain profitable.

TWA, one of Las Vegas's most successful airlines since 1930, reduced its number of daily flights from twenty-two to four in the 1980s, and then discontinued its service in the Las Vegas market in the 1990s because its international routes of Los Angeles to Paris and domestic transcontinental routes of San Francisco to New York were more profitable. This was a better business strategy for TWA, an airline whose fleet consisted mostly of wide-bodied Lockheed L-1011s and Boeing 747s, which could carry 300–400 passengers. According to Duane Busch, "It was never profitable for TWA to fly to Las Vegas; hence that is why we focused on and dominated the international market. A flight from New York to Paris brought in far more revenue than a flight from New York to Las Vegas. And many other airlines, such as United and American, also followed suit."[25] But some major airlines were able to weather the competition because they served enough markets where they could afford it.

Unlike TWA, United and American did not entirely eliminate their flights to Las Vegas. They were able to do this because the sheer volume of their business from the most profitable transcontinental routes of Los Angeles to New York or international routes of San Francisco to Paris made it possible for them to absorb the smaller profits in high-volume, low-yield leisure markets such as Las Vegas. Delta Airlines, a major Las Vegas air carrier, followed the same business strategy as United and American, offering twenty-two daily nonstop flights from Las Vegas to Atlanta, Cincinnati, Dallas, Los Angeles, Phoenix, and Salt Lake City. Servicing Las Vegas brought revenue for the airline, McCarran International Airport, and southern Nevada's economy.

Delta annually contributed more than $38.5 million to the area's economy, $3 million of which comprised employee salaries, takeoff and landing fees, and ticket counter and gate rentals at McCarran International Airport. According to Al Adams, Delta's district marketing manager, "Wherever Delta flies, its presence in the community helps spur a city's economic growth. Airport jobs create buying power, and airlines and airline-related businesses are important customers for goods and services by other firms. In addition, airlines bring businesspeople, vacationers, and conventioneers into a city," all of which in the case of Las Vegas mandated significant airport expansion.[26]

In 1974 McCarran International Airport officials had just completed a $30 million airport expansion project and were in the process of drafting plans for future expansion, which included lengthening runways, reinforcing and lengthening taxiways, providing more jetways, and expanding terminals. The onslaught of ten million air travelers, however, forced them to activate their plans right away. Handling so many travelers demanded close working relationships among the airlines, the airport, and the casino-resorts. McCarran, so conveniently located near the Strip, became the facilitator for the entire process. Robert Cohn, a partner with the airline legal firm Shaw, Pittman, Potts, and Trowbridge, pointed out that "airports should work hand-in-glove from the beginning with the airlines. Cities have to recognize the importance of air service to the economics of the community, and appreciate the economic power of the airport. It is the central nervous system of the economy. It enables the city to attract more commerce."[27] This was true of McCarran, which by 1998, along with the airlines, pumped more than $17 billion into the southern Nevada economy.[28]

After the Airline Deregulation Act of 1978 opened the floodgates for more planes, more flights, and more airport slots, and certainly more travelers, everything changed. Airport director John Solomon and his staff had to immediately revise and activate the master plan.

Solomon, formerly an assistant director of Tulsa Airport, and chairman of the U.S. Governmental Affairs Committee of the Airports Council International, acknowledged that the newly renovated airport was inadequate to meet the needs of an explosively growing airline industry and passenger volume: "By the time the industry stabilized, McCarran had approximately three times the number of air carriers previously serviced. We needed a terminal plan, to not only provide adequate service for seventeen existing airline tenants, but to additionally prepare us for anticipated future demands." Looking at the logistics of the new master plan, Solomon added, "We started working on roadways, a new satellite and a baggage claim building. Seven consulting firms and more than 1,000 persons were employed on the project."[29] Beginning the expansion was timely because the studies by Landrum and Brown and TRA Airport Consulting accurately predicted that ten million travelers would pass through McCarran's gates in 1980, but fell dramatically short when that number increased to twenty million in 1990 and to more than thirty million by 1996.[30]

Since this was the most ambitious expansion plan in the history of the airport and the city, the first problem was the cost. Phase I of "McCarran 2000" called for a third runway 5,000 feet in length, expansion of the existing terminal by 1,171,000 square feet for a total of 1,677,650 square feet to house 12 baggage claim carousels and 18 more gates, bringing the total to 54 gates. It also included plans for construction of a six-story parking structure with 3,526 parking spaces, new cargo facilities, a crash/fire/rescue facility, an air traffic control tower cab complete with radar for arriving and departing aircraft, and an automated transit system to shuttle passengers from the terminals to the gates. The cost of Phase I was $315 million, exceeding the initial projection of $276.6 million.[31] Through the Airport Development Aid Program, the federal government would pay $126 million of the cost, leaving the airport to bear the remaining $189 million, which it planned to pay with $1.3 million in slot machine revenue and $187.7 million in bonds and takeoff and landing fees assessed to the airlines.[32]

Phases II and III called for more airline ticket and rental car counter space, an expanded baggage claim area, and an enlarged parking structure of nine stories with the capacity to accommodate 6,500 automobiles and commercial vehicles, as well as a remote parking site for overflow. The plans also included construction of two more satellite concourses: Concourse C, with 16 gates for Southwest Airlines and Concourse D, with 26 gates for United,

American, Delta, and other airlines.[33] Phase III, which was unveiled in 1994, included plans for an airport connector and roadway system to give drivers easy access to the airport from Interstate 215.

With the increase in the number of airlines serving McCarran International Airport and the explosion in passenger volume as well as the construction of a second terminal for additional international flights, airport officials encountered significant problems with ground traffic congestion. Landrum and Brown's airport master plan took into account the heavy ground traffic that would result from the changes and offered solutions to resolve the issue. Widening Paradise Road and Tropicana Avenue, as well as building additional access roads and bypass roads to the terminals, would alleviate much of the congestion, especially during peak-hour traffic.

As early as 1975, marketing officials advised city officials to prepare for a boom in international tourism and travel, a market that could bring more profits to the airlines, the airport, the casino-resorts, and the city. Peter Ueberroth, president and chairman of the board of First Travel Corporation and the keynote speaker at a Sahara Hotel luncheon observing Nevada World Trade and Tourism Association Week, told local business leaders they could "fill hotels seven days a week if they [could] capture an exploding international tourist business." He predicted that "the amount of international travelers is going to overwhelm us."[34] Ueberroth encouraged local hotels to work with airlines and travel agencies to attract international travelers by lowering room rates, offering international flights to Las Vegas from other countries, and trying to get international travelers to fly during the week as well as on weekends. He cited statistics showing that tourism nationally generated $5 billion in 1970 and $11 billion in 1974.[35] Ueberroth's admonition was prescient. In the 1980s, a group of airports called U.S. Airports for Better International Air Service united to advance progress in bringing more foreign air carriers to the United States. This initiative would be called the "Open Skies Agreement."[36]

U.S. presidents, including Bill Clinton, long had sought to promote international air travel because of its profitability potential. In 1995 Clinton was able to broker an agreement with Canada, "deregulating the world's largest aviation market, [offering] more flights, and lower fares."[37] In 1998 he signed a bilateral agreement with Japan, creating a $10 billion market from annually transporting 12 million passengers and more than a billion pounds of cargo.[38] For Las Vegas, such agreements were vital to sustaining and growing the two primary industries upon which it depended for revenue: tourism and gambling. The city needed to tap more national and international markets, and the passenger plane helped it accomplish that goal.

According to McCarran Airport director Bob Broadbent, the Open Skies Agreement benefited the airport in many ways. First, the sheer number of visitors increased. For example, in 1985 international visitors accounted for 600,000 air travelers; a decade later that number jumped to nearly one million air travelers.[39] Additional benefits included revenue from takeoff and landing fees, jetway rental, ticket counter rental, cargo sales, and concession sales.

Part of what prompted the search for international travelers and airlines, said John Hanks, head of McCarran Airport's international marketing, was a conversation that had taken place between Kirk Kerkorian, owner of the MGM Grand, and Bob Broadbent. In 1986 Kerkorian approached Broadbent asking if his air travelers could fill MGM Grand's hotel rooms, to which Broadbent replied, "No, we need more flights."[40]

Broadbent's statement was important because it underscored what the airport needed to do to increase business and make Las Vegas better known globally: it needed to reach out to international air carriers. Over the next decade, by establishing partnerships with international airlines for nonstop flights, Hanks and his staff were able to add Toronto–to–Las Vegas flights on Air Canada, Tokyo–to–Las Vegas flights on Japan Airlines, London–to–Las Vegas flights on Virgin Atlantic, and Hermosillo–to–Las Vegas flights on AeroMexico.[41] These new flights opened Las Vegas to international markets that would provide more than 14 percent of McCarran's total air traveler volume. Manuel Cortez, president and CEO of the Las Vegas Convention and Visitors Authority, especially hailed the service from Tokyo as "a boon to the Japanese market in Las Vegas, which accounts for the second greatest number of overseas visitors."[42] Herald Bomberg, senior vice president of AeroMexico's U.S. operations, praised the Hermosillo–to–Las Vegas route as an opening "to the untapped Latin American market for Las Vegas, as the city becomes AeroMexico's 11th U.S. gateway." He added, "The new non-stop service will provide an important link for feed traffic from other Mexican cities."[43]

With increased international travel demand and more foreign airlines coming to Las Vegas, Bechtel Airport Contractors drafted blueprints for an international terminal with eight gates for use by Japan Airlines, Mexicana, AeroMexico, Canadian, Air Canada, Condor, Virgin Atlantic, and a screening area for U.S. Customs and Border Protection. The growing demand for international air travel prompted the Board of County Commissioners chairwoman, Thalia Dondero, to assert that an international terminal was needed because "it is not only possible, but highly probable that passengers, if offered the chance, would rather fly direct to Las Vegas from Japan, for example, than to Los Angeles or San Francisco since this is the ultimate destination for many of them."[44]

In 1998 the Las Vegas Convention and Visitors Authority, McCarran Airport, the Las Vegas Chamber of Commerce, the Nevada Resort Association, and the Nevada Development Authority united to form The Parties, whose responsibility was to focus on increasing both domestic and international air service to southern Nevada. According to Bill Mahaffey, manager of the Las Vegas Convention and Visitors Authority, "The role of the Las Vegas Parties is to counsel the airlines of the world on the opportunities available for expansion of existing service or to welcome new service to Las Vegas."[45] It was, however, not an easy task to open international markets and bring foreign airlines to Las Vegas—first, the federal government had to set up bilateral agreements with foreign countries to open their markets to international travel.

Once those agreements were established, international travel to Las Vegas increased dramatically. In 1990, 800,000 international air travelers came to the city. By 2000 that number increased to 1.2 million.[46] While the increase in international passengers was a boon to tourism and the internationally themed mega-resorts, airlines needed bigger jets to transport the larger numbers of air travelers, which meant substantial work on airport runways.

With many international airlines flying heavier wide-body aircraft to McCarran from Tokyo, Frankfurt, Toronto, and Seoul, especially Boeing 767s, Douglas DC-10s, and Airbus A-340s, the airport needed to lengthen and reinforce its existing runways and build new ones. Building another runway paralleling the north–south Runway 1-19 that would be 8,900 feet long and 150 feet wide, and extending a runway paralleling east–west Runway 7-25 would cost $87 million.[47] Other parts of the $500 million Phase IV expansion plan included a nine-story parking structure for 8,000 automobiles, lengthened ticket counters, four more baggage carousels in Terminal 1, and a tunnel under the east–west runways to link Interstate 215 to the airport. The plan also allowed space for more concessions in Concourses A and B, a pilots' lounge, a customer service center, a restaurant with a balcony view, stores, more restaurants, slot machines, and other revenue producers. The concourse's walls and ceiling would be made of 66,000 square feet of glass to give people in the facility an unobstructed view of the airport and the desert. The floor would consist of 130,000 square feet of imported Italian marble. With the opening of the D gates in 1997, the most recent round of renovations enabled McCarran to handle up to 45 million passengers annually.[48]

To get to the Concourse C and Concourse D gates from the terminal, travelers rode an Automated Transit System tram. Additionally, the airport built a $4 million, 78,500-square-foot warehouse to handle more than 200 million pounds of cargo.[49] Getting contracts with new passenger airlines often depended on McCarran's ability to handle cargo, since low-yield markets prompted airlines to supplement their income by also transporting freight. With the rapid expansion of the air cargo market and many carriers looking for new locations to increase air service and have access to land routes in more heavily populated areas, Las Vegas was ideally situated to become a major West Coast cargo distribution center.

The airport also profited financially from the Foreign Trade Zone (FTZ), an area on the airport's periphery that allowed international importers duty-free storage and assembly of foreign products tax free. The FTZ originally consisted of a 120,000-square-foot warehouse on 160 acres with an adjunct 25 acres of land for development and FTZ use. The FTZ was a boon not only to the airport but also to the city in that it helped diversify the economy of the metropolitan area, and it benefited the resorts by easing the pressure to raise gaming taxes. More important, the FTZ stimulated free trade, increased cargo business, and enticed businesses such as Ocean Spray, Levi Strauss, Service Merchandise, and other international companies to move their headquarters to Las Vegas.[50]

The Foreign Trade Zone also inspired the Board of County Commissioners to look into a foreign trade center, which would consist of a five-story building totaling 1,700,000 square feet of display space, an international services area, a restaurant, and meeting areas, all for a price of $190 million.[51] But once again, rapid growth created space problems. The airport's planned enlargement of FTZ facilities was still inadequate. By the late 1990s, as the passenger volume steadily surged toward McCarran's maximum capacity of 55 million travelers, officials realized that further expansion would be necessary.

In 1999 airport planners conducted a study and concluded that the construction of a second major airport would be necessary to alleviate McCarran's air traffic and terminal congestion problems. In a letter to the chairman of the House Transportation and Infrastructure Subcommittee on Aviation, Clark County director of aviation Randall Walker illustrated the airport's desperate need for land. He explained that there were more than 550,000 air-craft operations (aircraft movement on the ground) annually at an airport whose maximum capacity was 705,000, a figure that would easily be reached by 2013. Walker estimated that without expansion the average flight would be delayed by at least twenty minutes, costing commercial airlines and char-ter carriers more than $1,000 per delay. He feared that the added expense might discourage airlines from offering more flights to Las Vegas and lead them to seek more-profitable markets elsewhere.[52]

But because Las Vegas had become a major business and tourist center and had federal government subsidies for transporting mail, airlines did not have to worry about empty seats. Passenger volume rose steadily each year, and more travelers began to book connecting flights through McCarran. Since Las Vegas, like Orlando, had been a final destination for air travelers for years, the concept of connecting flights in Las Vegas on Southwest and America West Airlines was a new idea. But with the city's better year-round weather and an efficient air traffic control system already in place, McCarran soon became a connecting flight airport for millions of passengers. Predict-ably, the increase in flights put more pressure on airport officials to expand the airport. In his letter, Walker indicated that the airport had already reached its 2,400-acre capacity and had only enough room for "short and mid-term growth." He noted that during peak periods, Las Vegas air traffic controllers handled more than 120 arrivals and departures per hour and that any additional flights would saturate the system. He also mentioned that since 1990 passenger traffic had increased by 75 percent.[53] In 1998, 30,227,287 travelers passed through McCarran's gates; one year later, that number had increased to 33,669,185.[54]

By decade's end, air travel had become the most popular mode of trans-portation for tourists to southern Nevada, surpassing the automobile. It was "the lifeblood of Las Vegas," said Duane Busch, TWA executive station manager. "Without it, the city would not enjoy even half of the revenue tour-ists bring."[55] But the golden age of air travel to Las Vegas really began when the passenger volume between 1980 and 1990 doubled from ten million to twenty million. Eight years later it surpassed thirty million and in 2000, nearly reached forty million.[56] It must be remembered that the airline indus-try made the growth and development of Las Vegas possible as a unique American model of the twenty-first-century city through a highly developed system of delivering business, leisure, and resident air travelers to McCarran International Airport, and to the casino-resorts. While many Las Vegas historians and urban scholars attribute the growth and development of the city to gambling, tourism, favorable weather, and a relaxed tax infrastructure—all of which no doubt were a part of it—the main catalyst was the airlines. With the airlines bringing so many passengers to McCarran Airport, airport planners and officials hoped that all of their renovated facilities, now including 93 gates, would be sufficient to accommodate more than 28 million passengers by 1990 until plans could be drawn for a more comprehensive airport expansion plan in the twenty-first century. To help pay for current expansion costs, the airport charged a $3 passenger facility fee and a 10 percent tax on all airline tickets.[57] In the meantime, Walker requested more money for a much-discussed new airport.

In 2001, with federal funds becoming available for a new airport near Ivanpah and help from influential Nevada senators Harry Reid and John Ensign, airport officials devised a new plan to secure additional moneys for McCarran to alleviate its congestion and prepare the facility to handle its maximum capacity. The centerpiece of "Vision 2020" was a new airport south of Las Vegas. Despite opposition from environmentalists, who argued that arrival and departure routes crossing over the Mojave National Preserve would cause excessive damage, the county received approval from the Bureau of Land Management to purchase 6,500 acres of land thirty miles south of the Las Vegas Valley for $13 million. When construction of the new airport was completed in 2013, it would handle cargo and international flights, in addition to overflow of scheduled commercial flights to McCarran. Dennis Mewshaw, planning manager for the Clark County Department of Aviation, estimated that two to four million passengers would pass through the new airport's gates by the end of its first year in operation. The first phase of construction, which was slated to begin in 2005, included a terminal building, one runway, and surface parking and carried a price tag of $1.5 billion to $2 billion.[58]

In addition to the new airport in Ivanpah, other stages of the plan that were already under way included more airline ticket counter space and baggage claim carousels at McCarran's main terminal, a third wing added to Concourse D, which provided ten more gates, and construction of a $770 million third terminal that would have its own parking garage, ticket counters, and baggage claim facilities with 14 gates, 8 of which were reserved for international air carrier use. The airport also built an off-site 80,000-square-foot, $120 million facility for all rental car companies, thus making space available for the new baggage claim carousels, and a new air traffic control tower.[59]

Future phases of the plan included provisions for the improvement of other Clark County airports. To handle more private planes and air tour carrier services, North Las Vegas Airport would receive a third runway, a new apron, more hangar facilities, and a new air traffic control tower. Henderson Executive Airport would be funded for construction of a new terminal building, a second parallel runway, a new apron, and more shade hangars. The plans also included construction of a fourth terminal at McCarran providing 15 more gates, thus allowing the airport to meet its goal of 120 gates. Excluding the new airport, all of the additional expansion outlined in "Vision 2020" would cost $1.26 billion.[60] According to Hilarie Grey, public affairs manager for the Clark County Department of Aviation, federal airport improvement funds and airport revenue would finance the project, along with $385 million in municipal bonds at a 6.32 percent interest rate.[61]

Airport officials and the Board of County Commissioners desperately needed the land in Ivanpah. McCarran Airport had no further room for significant expansion of any kind. It could not risk upsetting the airlines, which, along with the airport, in 1998 directly and indirectly contributed $17 billion to the southern Nevada economy. Airport officials clearly recognized the urgency and the significance of the issue, saying that "nearly half of all Las Vegas visitors arrive by air via McCarran International Airport, highlighting the important connection between the tourism industry and airport demand. In fact, growth in passenger volume has been so closely linked to the construction of new hotel rooms that statistical analysis reveals that for each 10,000 rooms that open in Las Vegas, 3.5 million additional passengers used McCarran."[62] Las Vegas had twenty-one airlines and an expanded international airport, but it needed mega-accommodations with the resort hotels on the Strip for record numbers of arriving national and international air travelers as part of the forty million visitors who journeyed to Las Vegas every year, especially during the last two decades of the century. This enormous influx of visitors prompted the new mega-resort movement.

The mega-resort movement got its start in 1989 with pioneer Steve Wynn's Mirage, a massive Polynesian-themed $750 million property with 3,044 rooms, a volcano with pyrotechnics, a lagoon, waterfalls, a 20,000-gallon saltwater coral reef aquarium (behind the registration desk), eight private bungalows, six swimming pools, twelve restaurants, a dolphin habitat, and the famous Siegfried and Roy with their white Bengal tiger shows, which drew thousands of awestruck tourists.[63]

Wynn, the son of a bingo parlor owner, got his start in the casino industry in Las Vegas as part owner of the Frontier Hotel and as owner of Standard Liquor Distribution. His liquor distribution company, which serviced many of the casinos, gave him the opportunity to learn about the casino business firsthand through his friendships with the old and new casino owners. Wynn's ambitions did not stop with redesigning and refurbishing old casinos. He was determined to build a property that was bigger than Kirk Kerkorian's International and Landmark, and Jay Sarno's Caesars Palace. According to Las Vegas historians Eugene Moehring and Michael Green, Wynn's Mirage "boasted not only size and elegance, but also the special attractions that separated the Strip from Fremont Street, Reno, other Nevada Resorts, and every gambling town, tribal casino, and Internet Web site in the world."[64] Wynn set the bar higher than his predecessors in his effort to accommodate every visitor's needs and provide the ultimate tourist experience, and it was up to his competitors to rise to his level.

The next year, 1990, William Bennett, owner of Circus Circus, a lower-end property that catered to families, built a more elegant resort, the 4,032-room Excalibur, themed after King Arthur and the Knights of the Round Table and featuring a castle and a moat. This mega-resort contained a 100,000-square-foot casino, thirteen restaurants, several of which were buffets with service for families, an arena with knights engaging in jousting matches, a theater for family entertainment, a large swimming pool, and a spa. Bennett followed Excalibur with the middle-income Luxor, an Egyptian-themed, actual-size pyramid resort surrounded by beautiful gardens filled with Egyptian statuary. This mega-resort had 2,526 rooms, a 120,000-square-foot casino, a swimming pool, a spa, a showroom, a movie theater, an entertainment lounge, a replica of King Tut's tomb, and fourteen restaurants, all built at a cost of $375 million.[65]

In 1993 Kirk Kerkorian built the new MGM Grand (the old one had suffered fire damage), the world's largest high-rise mega-resort, to challenge Wynn's Mirage. The Emerald City, Wizard of Oz–themed mega-resort sat on 112 acres of land, contained 5,005 rooms in a massive thirty-story tower, a 171,500-square-foot casino, parking for 6,000 automobiles, an entire sports casino (including gaming book), twenty-three retail shops, five lounges and bars, eight restaurants, a 30,000-square-foot video arcade for children, a 144,000-square-foot swimming pool area with a beach, a 34-acre theme park complete with rides, a 380,000-square-foot conference center, and a monorail connecting the resort to Bally's hotel. This property, like the Mirage, was designed to be all-inclusive so visitors would not need to leave it.[66]

Other mega-resorts included the Bellagio and the Venetian, which simulated Venice with visitor-filled gondolas floating along artificial canals. This mega-resort had 3,036 rooms, elegant international shops and fine restaurants, and 500,000 square feet of convention space. The Paris's amenities included 2,916 hotel rooms, a 140,000-square-foot convention center, an 85,000-square-foot casino, and a giant replica of the Eiffel Tower, all at a construction cost of $760 million. The new, redesigned Aladdin, an $826 million Arabian Desert–themed resort with 2,567 rooms, a 115,000-square-foot casino, and a 426,000-square-foot shopping mall opened in 2000 and immediately became a tourist favorite.[67]

Off the Strip, the Latin-themed Rio Hotel opened in January 1999 with 2,000 hotel rooms, a 102,000-square-foot showroom complex, a 1,500-seat state-of-the-art theater, and a 110,000-square-foot entertainment and convention complex. Wanda Chan, director of hotel operations, commented that there indeed was a symbiotic relationship between the airlines and the casinos: "They went hand in hand."[68] The mega-resorts depended on the airlines to bring business in the form of tourists, gamblers, conventioneers, and business travelers. And the airlines depended on the resorts to provide an attractive destination for their passengers. According to Chan, package deals "had a decent-sized" impact on the hotel, but the greater impact was convention attendance.[69]

Randall Walker agreed with Chan: "The airport has a symbiotic relationship with the hotel industry. It responds to growth in the hotel industry," or sometimes vice versa.[70] According to Walker, one hotel room annually meant 350 passengers. In 1989 Las Vegas reported an 89.8 percent hotel room occupancy rate for the mega-resorts, and just over 17 million air travelers passed through McCarran's gates. In 1993 the hotel occupancy rate increased by 3 percent to 92.8 percent, and passenger volume at McCarran rose to 22 million.[71]

These hotel occupancy rates and passenger volume statistics reflected the broader national trend of the effects of airline deregulation combined with lower airfares, a growing consumer movement, increased public affluence, especially during the Clinton years with the longest economic boom in U.S. history, a growing U.S. population, and more public interest in national and international travel. For Las Vegas they indicated "the kind of explosive growth that few American cities have ever experienced. For all of the 1990s and into the twenty-first century, Las Vegas was the fastest growing metropolitan area in the nation."[72] The airlines were the vital link that enabled this growth to happen. Bill Mahaffey, Delta Airlines district marketing manager, said as much: "The changes which have come to Las Vegas and Delta in the years since the airline became part of the city's life [1961] have been marked by a common denominator: healthy, well-founded progress. Las Vegas and Delta have both gained world recognition. Both have greatly contributed to each other." Mahaffey added, "The past 25 years have been good to Las Vegas and Delta. The city has continued to increase in importance as one of the world's major convention and tourist centers."[73]

The end of the twentieth century was boom time for the resort city in the desert, with record numbers of global air travelers, an expanded airport, and ten new mega-resorts on the Strip offering a smorgasbord of entertainment venues, fine dining, and lavish room accommodations. The future looked endlessly bright, brimming with optimism, but it was not without growing pains. The airlines experienced turbulent times of unprecedented competition; crippling fuel costs; high labor costs, including wages, strikes, and pension payouts; debt from expensive aircraft leases; growing passenger discontent; and marginal profits, leading to mergers and bankruptcies. McCarran International Airport faced problems of air and ground traffic congestion, insufficient land for expansion, and costly airline delays resulting from the overcrowded air corridor 30,000 feet above the airport. The colossal resort hotels, among them the largest in the nation, needed still more guests to fill their many rooms. Resort executives turned to the airlines to add more flights and thereby to bring in more people.

David Ehlers, chairman of Las Vegas Investment Advisors, "long believed that the problem with Las Vegas visitor counts is not a lack of demand, but a lack of capacity to bring visitors here."[74] The growing pains were caused primarily by the mounting problems of a beleaguered airline industry, soon to be severely damaged by the terrorist attacks of September 11, 2001, which would endanger the symbiotic relationship between the airlines, the airport, and the city.

Following the attacks on the World Trade Center and the Pentagon, the U.S. airline industry halted all flights for one week. Airports were filled with jets idly parked at gates, remote locations, and anywhere else where there was room. Air traffic control radar screens were blank. Millions of travelers stranded at airports desperately sought ways to get home. Residents living near airports for the first time heard the rare sound of silence. The security of the country was in a state of national emergency, with the airlines and airports at the heart of it. Nobody knew when or how the airlines would resume operations, but it was certain that there would be major repercussions throughout the entire air travel industry.

Airliner hijackings and terrorism did not begin with the September 11 attack. In 1969 hijackers commandeered a TWA Boeing 707 from California and forced it to land in Rome. On March 8, 1972, after TWA Flight 57, a Boeing 707, landed at McCarran Airport and the crew and passengers deplaned, it was moved to a remote site for inspection in response to a bomb threat called in by an extortionist. A bomb planted in the rear of the cockpit exploded. There were no injuries and the perpetrator was never caught. In 1988 a Pan Am Boeing 747 with 259 passengers on board was hijacked and exploded over Lockerbie, Scotland, killing everyone on board.[75] All of these shocking events prompted very strict security measures at airports nationwide. On November 16, 1990, President George H. W. Bush signed the Aviation Security Improvement Act, mandating greater availability of resources to tighten and enforce security at the nation's commercial airports.[76] On October 9, 1996, President Bill Clinton signed the Federal Aviation Reauthorization Act, part of which included $1 billion for 54 state-of-the-art bomb diction units, 100 bomb-sniffing dog teams, and authorization for the Federal Aviation Administration to hire 300 special agents.[77] Guidelines established after 9/11 were even stricter.

Passengers were required to be at airports two hours in advance of their departure time, and terminals were heavily guarded by armed security personnel with bomb-sniffing dogs. After receiving boarding passes at the ticket counter, passengers advanced to long lines at security checkpoints to have their luggage inspected, and then they themselves had to move forward and pass through metal detectors. The Federal Aviation Administration, from time to time, tested the effectiveness of the screening process by secretly sending armed staff through the checkpoints. The entire process became a miserable hassle for passengers, but was a deadly serious situation for airline security. Historian David Courtwright observed: "Metal detectors and spot inspection weeded out the amateurs who lost their nerve and ditched their weapon in airport trashcans. But they failed to stop determined terrorists who studied security weaknesses and who were willing to go down with their planes. Precisely because air transport was so vital to the American economy, it remained the priority target."[78]

The financial implications of the September 11 attacks were catastrophic nationally for several airlines, including those servicing Las Vegas. Midway, United Shuttle, and National Airlines, in massive debt from high fuel prices, poor management, and now a rapidly declining passenger volume as a result of the public's fear of flying after 9/11, went out of business. The entire U.S. airline industry went into an economic tailspin. America West Airlines faced bankruptcy for a second time as its stock plummeted more than 65 percent, to $2.60 per share; United Airlines stock fell 40 percent, to $18.71 per share; Delta's, 41 percent, to $21.82 per share; American's, 39 percent, to $18.11 per share; and Southwest's, 22 percent, to $13.33 per share.[79] Not only did stock values decline, but most of the airlines had to reduce flight operations and slash thousands of jobs.

America West had to reduce its flight operations by 20 percent and elimi-nate 2,000 jobs. United Airlines, US Airways, and Continental Airlines com-bined cut more than 46,000 jobs.[80] Nationwide, passenger traffic declined by more than 50 percent as the airlines faced their biggest losses in nine years. Delta Airlines reported 30 percent of its daily flights full, and Northwest Air-lines only 59 percent; the airlines needed 65 percent of their seats filled to break even. That year, Delta lost $734 million and United lost nearly $1 bil-lion. By the end of fiscal year 2001, the airline industry had lost a total of $9 billion, an unprecedented amount for one year in the industry's history, and a continued trend of losing money dating to the early 1980s.[81]

Airline insurance rates sharply increased, forcing a rise in fares to cover insurance costs and additional fuel surcharge fees. From June 30, 2001, to June 30, 2002, economic liabilities jumped to $117.3 billion, a 20 percent increase.[82] As a result, the airlines had to ground planes, reduce the num-ber of flights, and even seriously consider merging. Essentially, the industry's future looked bleak, forcing air travelers to choose other modes of travel.

In Las Vegas, the Federal Aviation Administration, in immediate response to the terror attacks, grounded all arriving and departing flights at McCar-ran for an indefinite period of time. With no new air travelers coming to Las Vegas, officials of Caesars Palace, Paris, Bellagio, and other mega-resorts reported that within one week, room occupancy had declined to 60 percent, and they estimated gaming revenue losses to be in the tens of millions.[83] Consequently, hotel executives ordered that thousands of employees be laid off and canceled shows because of the sparse ticket sales. Retail shops in the Forum, Desert Passage, and Showcase Mall experienced enormous revenue losses. Taxicab companies eliminated dozens of cabdriver jobs after business declined by at least 50 percent. For the first time in six decades, Las Vegas went into a recession.

The terrorist attacks, bringing air travel to a halt, clearly demonstrated the dependency of a large national and international tourist industry on commercial airlines for transportation to resort cities such as Las Vegas, Miami, and Orlando. In Las Vegas, however, where tourism was a primary industry of the metropolitan area, the dependency on commercial airlines to bring in tourists was vital to the city's economy. Clark County commissioner Bruce Woodbury unequivocally admitted this when he said, "McCarran Airport [including the airlines] is the absolute heart of our tourism industry and economy."[84] With fewer tourists and less gaming revenue, the city would have had to raise taxes on the casinos and its residents to revive the economy, a move that would have angered parsimonious Las Vegans, who loathed paying taxes.

Following the attack, Clark County director of aviation Randall Walker commented: "Things will never be the same as they were before."[85] By the end of September, McCarran Airport had lost $5 million, concessions lost $635,000, and slot machine concessions lost $648,000. Only ticketed passengers were allowed to enter concourses, which hurt local business. Also, airport insurance increased from $700,000 a year to more than $2 million, and many passengers traveling to Los Angeles who had to wait in long lines to pass through security at McCarran decided to travel by automobile.[86] The malaise that permeated Las Vegas was eerily similar to the tenuous and depressing feeling among the townspeople during the 1922 Union Pacific railroad strike and economic recession.

By 2001, Las Vegas had become a world-class tourist destination. The luxurious passenger jets, user-friendly airport, amenity-filled mega-resorts, and rapidly growing city annually attracted more than forty million tourists, businesspeople, conventioneers, and gamblers. United, American, Delta, Northwest, Southwest, Continental, and other airlines enjoyed full flights and sustainable profits despite the low-yield Las Vegas market. The airlines had become vital to the sustenance and future geographic, economic, and cultural growth of Las Vegas. The September 11 attacks, however, threatened to severely weaken the symbiotic relationships enjoyed by the airlines, the airport, and the city. The *Las Vegas Review-Journal* commented: "Southern Nevada's dependence on air travel has led to slumping hotel room occupancy rates, and thousands of layoffs at Las Vegas area casinos."[87] In an opinion-editorial piece, *Las Vegas Sun* journalist Tony Cook argued, "Tourism is southern Nevada's most important industry. Economic growth largely depends on the region's ability to fly people in."[88] The effects of the September 11 terrorist attacks were more severe for Las Vegas with its dependence on the airlines than for its northern tourist and gaming competitor, Reno, where visitors mainly arrived by car. As long as McCarran International Airport remained a parking lot for passenger jets, the airlines, the airport, and the mega-resorts would lose hundreds of thousands of dollars daily.

With the September 11 attacks, the airlines, the airport, and the mega-resorts faced a new problem: passengers' fear of flying. According to *Las Vegas Sun* journalist David Strow, "The only way Las Vegas will return to its pre–September 11 levels is through increased demand—and that will happen only when American and international visitors feel comfortable flying again."[89] Jason Ader, an analyst with Bear Stearns, said, "People are starting to feel more confident. But business travel remains soft, and that is economy driven. The leisure market has to feel comfortable things are safe. That is just going to take time to heal."[90]

Historically, Las Vegas has always been a city that could reinvent itself even under the most adverse conditions. Recovery from the September 11 attacks would require the city to work harder than many other cities to bring the tourist business, its mainstay, back to pre–September 11 levels. Las Vegas set out to solve the problem by building even larger and more grandiose mega-resorts, with exotic luxury suites, lavishly designed casinos with more private gaming rooms, more five-star restaurants, and expensive box seat tickets to entertainment venues and sporting events, all designed and arranged to attract more higher-end domestic and international tourists and gamblers, who Steve Wynn, Sheldon Adelson, and other mega-resort magnates believed would spend more money. Though air travel remained important, the airlines, instead of promoting the excitement and sense of adventure with flight, serving delicious meals, and providing more gratis services, shifted the focus to the destination to attract more business and leisure passengers.

Still Growing During Tough Times

*D*espite 171,960 fewer air travelers in 2002 as a result of the 9/11 terrorist attacks, within one year the numbers of air travelers and visitors coming to Las Vegas rose higher than ever. In 2003, 36,265,932 passengers arrived by air, and in 2004, that number increased to 41,441,531. By 2007, 47,729,527 people arrived by plane.[1] From 1998 to 2007, the amount of money generated by visitors rose from $24,577,499,000 to $41,578,079,000, an increase of more than 40 percent.[2] Historians Eugene Moehring and Michael Green attribute the continued growth of Las Vegas to tourism, urban sprawl, and gambling, but missing from this explanation is the fact that the airlines were a powerful catalyst in driving the growth as they continued to bring ever larger numbers of tourists and gamblers to the desert resort city. Though the Las Vegas market remained lucrative for the airlines, nationally and internationally the industry still experienced significant problems.

Since the 1978 Airline Deregulation Act, the economic state of the U.S. airline industry had progressively declined, approaching near collapse and becoming a serious threat to the nation's economy and certainly to cities, such as Las Vegas, that depended on tourist-based economies. High fuel prices, deep debt, increased competition, and poor management increased the airline industry's volatility. With such a heavy dependence on the airlines for business, and given that Las Vegas was a low-yield leisure travel market (meaning that airlines made less profit because of low fares resulting from high competition), there was always the possibility that Las Vegas might lose air carrier service, especially after the 9/11 attacks.

In 2002 America West, Las Vegas's second-biggest airline, reported a loss of $347 million in the first quarter. The airline had to cut ten of its daily flights serving Las Vegas from New York, Phoenix, and Washington, D.C.[3] Southwest Airlines, the largest carrier serving Las Vegas, saw a passenger decrease of 4.8 percent and reduced its daily flights at McCarran from 169 to

125.[4] That same year, United Airlines lost $2.97 billion, the largest annual loss in airline industry history, and had to declare bankruptcy for the first time in its own history. United's restructuring plan of frugality pressured all union staff—pilots, flight attendants, mechanics, and customer service agents—to agree to a 30 percent pay cut. Further, the airline retired one hundred of its aged jets—Boeing 727s, 737s, and DC-10s—and replaced them with more-efficient jets such as the Airbus A319 and A320 and the Boeing 757 and 767 to save money on fuel and other costs. The company also cut 10 percent of its domestic flights. The fifth-largest airline nationwide watched its passenger volume in Las Vegas drop by 21.2 percent. Even with the restructuring, which included the need to reduce wages by $2.4 billion per year through 2008, the airline still lost $3.2 billion in 2002. United left bankruptcy with $17 billion in debt and received $3 billion in exit financing secured with weak mortgages on all of the airline's assets.[5]

Delta and American did not fare any better. Facing massive debt and bankruptcy, Delta had to ground forty planes and cut domestic capacity by 10 percent.[6] American followed suit, having lost a total of $5.2 billion from 2001 to 2002, forcing CEO Don Carty to resign, and the airline had to cut 189 daily flights and 12 percent of its domestic capacity nationwide.[7] In the first three months of 2002, all of the U.S. airlines lost a combined $2.4 billion and were on course to lose another $6.4 billion. By the end of that year, long-term debt for the airlines increased from $15 billion to $43.2 billion, the highest ever.[8]

Recognizing that the airlines were drowning in debt and facing economic collapse, in 2001 Congress already had passed the Air Transportation Safety and System Stabilization Act, an emergency $5 billion loan to keep troubled airlines afloat. But the airlines needed more money. Knowing how vital air travel was to the country and its economy, Congress was not going to let them go out of business. That outcome would have been devastating to the country, especially to leisure travel markets like Orlando and Las Vegas that heavily depended on the airlines to bring business. United received $1.8 billion in government loans to help ease its economic crisis. Delta received $600 million, and America West was given $380 million.[9] But this loan money did not last long, as the airlines continued to rapidly burn through the cash to pay down their massive debt, which included pensions, aircraft leases, and high fuel costs.

In 2005 Continental Airlines grounded sixty-seven planes and slashed 3,000 jobs nationwide.[10] Sky West, a usually profitable regional Las Vegas commuter airline, saw its profits decline by 27 percent. Editorialists nationwide warned that the airline industry would continue to lose billions of dollars before anything could improve. *St. Louis Post-Dispatch* editorial writer Tim McLaughlin warned: "Despite shedding billions of dollars in labor and pension costs since 2000, U.S. airlines will need to cut billions more before the end of the decade to make money and remain competitive."[11] Anthony Sabino, a St. John's University law professor, echoed McLaughlin's gloomy outlook, asserting that "barring a miraculous recovery—cheap oil, massive increase in travel or the low-cost carriers disappearing, one, if not two, of these legacy carriers will disappear via merger or liquidation."[12] The impact of a merger would mean reduced flight capacity, higher fares, a greater possibility of labor issues or financial crises, a loss of service in certain communities, greater difficulty for new upstart airlines to enter markets to increase competition and lower fares, and a decline in the quality of customer service. An airline forced to go out of business, such as Pan Am, meant less service for air travelers, and the loss of 24,000 jobs. The situation was a potentially ominous sign for McCarran Airport, the casino-resorts, and the city of Las Vegas, all of which depended on the airlines to bring tourists and gamblers. The casino-resorts and the city had to figure out a way to continue attracting tourists, which they did through cheaper package deals, more shops, and more-diverse entertainment venues. It was not so easy for the airlines.

Desperately trying to minimize loss and launch some kind of recovery, the major airlines took serious steps to control costs. Delta, Continental, Northwest, and American, like United, all demanded tough cost-saving measures, including cutting into employee salaries and deferring benefits. The unions threatened pickets and strikes, but to no avail, forcing them to save the airlines by reluctantly accepting management's demands, which included salary cuts, less-comprehensive medical benefits, and reduced pension payouts. United and US Airways attempted to merge, but United's pilots opposed the merger, not wanting to assume US Air's own financial problems and take on the difficult task of integrating seniority lists to match pay scales.[13]

All airlines continued to downgrade their gas-guzzling mid-size jets, the Boeing 737 and the Airbus A319, to smaller ones such as the Bombardier and the Canadair, regional jets with seating for 50 to 100 passengers. Though these aircraft were much smaller than their counterparts, they still flew at the same altitudes, speeds, and distances as the larger jets and were more fuel-efficient. The sacrifice of downgrading for passengers was smaller seats in crowded cabins and fewer services. In 2001 regional jets replaced 732 larger planes, and by 2013 the number of regional jets in operation is projected to be 2,970.[14] Most airlines also assessed their markets to discern which were the most profitable and then moved their fleets there. As a result, according to Mark Suman, cofounder of Las Vegas–based National Airlines, "Planes may be moved to routes where they can serve more business customers. Business customers are more profitable to airlines than leisure travelers because they tend to book more expensive last-minute flights." He added, "Las Vegas is competing with other cities when it comes to aircraft allocation and the economics put the city at a disadvantage."[15] Even these cost-saving measures, however, had limited impact because many of the airlines still were too deep in debt and struggling to break even.

Southwest Airlines and Allegiant Airlines, two discount carriers with less debt than the other major carriers, managed to turn a profit by 2003. Southwest earned revenue of $511 million.[16] The airline's chief executive officer, Herb Kelleher, had the ideal business model: keep fares low, offer service to smaller cities where other airlines did not fly, have one class of seating, and compensate employees adequately. Like many other discount carriers, Southwest not only enjoyed profitability but saw much of its market grow as the "Big Six" airlines—American, United, Continental, Delta, Northwest, and US Air—reduced their numbers of flights and service to cities. In May 1992 the Big Six controlled 72 percent of the airline market, while regional airlines controlled 11 percent and discounters 10 percent. In May 2002 the Big Six controlled 56 percent, regional carriers 15 percent, and discounters 23 percent.[17] One editorial writer opined that discounters would control even more of the airline market in the future: "Low fare airlines gravitating toward secondary airports were likely to fare better than the major airlines because at secondary airports, there was less air traffic congestion and lower airport user fees would keep the costs down."[18] In fiscal year 2003–2004, Southwest was in such demand, transporting 5,904,426 passengers to and from McCarran International Airport, that it established a third hub in Las Vegas.[19]

Allegiant Airlines, a Las Vegas–based low-cost airline, earned a profit of $132 million and added additional flights to Las Vegas from all of the cities the airline served. Allegiant followed Southwest's strategy: fly one type of plane and serve outlying airports. The airline flew McDonnell Douglas MD-80s, 140-passenger jets able to fly at an altitude of 37,000 feet and a speed exceeding 500 miles per hour. Because of the airline's affordable fares and accommodating flight schedules to second- and third-tier cities and airports, in 2004 the airline was on track to earn $265 million in revenue the next fiscal year.[20]

For leisure travelers and, more broadly, the Las Vegas market, discount airlines like Southwest, Allegiant, and JetBlue remained popular because they kept fares low. In June 2005, 3.8 million passengers came to Las Vegas.[21] Of that record number, Southwest Airlines transported more than 1.2 million, America West 697,387, Northwest Airlines, 144,070, Jet Blue 77,126, Allegiant 70,754, and Frontier 38,496—all double-digit percentage increases over the same month of the previous year.[22] West Jet, a low-cost international carrier, increased its number of daily nonstop flights from nine Canadian destinations to ten, and Singapore Airlines offered three weekly flights on Boeing 777s, which brought an additional 3,000 international travelers each month to McCarran Airport.[23] In 2007 the air travel volume in Las Vegas reached its peak, with 47,728,414 passengers, indicative of a thriving high-volume market.[24] For the right price, people still were willing to come to Las Vegas for fun and sun, but they did not spend as much money as they had in previous years, when the nation's economy was better.

The airlines also had to figure out ways to further reduce costs. To cut costs, the airlines used one-third fewer wide-body jets for the 143 daily transcontinental flights in the United States. They also directed pilots to fly slower, to conserve fuel. With fuel at $3.54 per gallon, airlines in 2008 expected to pay $61.2 billion, more than $20 billion more than the previous year's total cost.[25]

The U.S. domestic airline market was not the only part of the industry suffering from high fuel prices. Globally, non-U.S. airlines lost $5.2 billion, prompting Giovanni Bisignani, director general and CEO of the International Air Transportation Association, which represents 230 airlines and 94 percent of the world's passenger and cargo flights, to call for a meeting in Istanbul, Turkey, at which he noted: "The industry is in crisis, perhaps the biggest crisis we've ever faced."[26] But U.S. airlines were in worse shape. With a declining dollar and fuel costs accounting for 36 percent of an airline's operating expenses, U.S. carriers took the biggest hit, despite operating the greatest number of planes in the world and receiving continued government subsidies to transport mail. With an ailing airline industry, an article in *USA Today* noted, "resorts, hotels, cruise lines, and convention destinations could suffer. Tourism, especially in states like Florida, Hawaii, and Nevada that depend on [the airline industry] heavily, could take a hit damaging state economies and forcing cuts in government services."[27]

With the growing distress and damage caused by the recession, the mega-resorts and the airport in Las Vegas turned to the airlines with two immediate options: bring more domestic passengers to Las Vegas and hope that they would spend more money as the recession waned, or focus on the international airlines and tourists who may have more time and money for travel. Mega-resort executives and airport officials chose to pursue the latter option.

At a press conference, Clark County Department of Aviation director Randall Walker explained the importance of Las Vegas's bid to attract more international airlines: "International travelers spend an average of $500 more per day than a typical domestic traveler, and the non-gaming effect of one fully-loaded jumbo jet is about $200,000—roughly $75 million annually with daily flights."[28] Since 1968, McCarran had been an international airport, with Hughes Air West offering flights from Las Vegas to destinations in Canada and Mexico, and over the next four decades the airport had reached out to other members of the international market to acquire fourteen new airlines, covering Europe, Asia, and Central America. As a result, it not only increased the number of international travelers from 1 million in 2000 to more than 2.3 million in 2009, but connected Las Vegas to other major international cities such as Paris, Rome, London, Seoul, and Manila.[29]

Following the 9/11 attacks, airport officials suspended all but the most crucial expansion plans and reconfigured the lower concourses that housed the ticket counters and airport offices to make room for bomb-detection machines. The added expense of the security equipment and a decrease in revenue resulting in fewer flights and passengers exacerbated McCarran's economic problems. The airport had considerable debt from previous expansion projects, including $360 million outstanding in service bonds and $1.3 billion in subordinated bonds. Inadequate revenue from parking fees, retail concessions, and airline-related fees (airlines accounted for 35 percent of the airport's revenue), caused officials to worry that the airport might default on its debts.[30]

The airport also delayed further expansion because of the serious problems facing airlines in general: high jet fuel prices, a failing national economy, and the possibility that some of the major carriers could go bankrupt or out of business. McCarran had to postpone a $348 million phase of its $4 billion expansion project, which included $10 million for a new elevator and escalator system, $114.5 million for a new heliport south of town, and $215 million for reconstruction of Runway 25R. The airport also had to postpone installation of new curbside signs ($6 million) and improvements to the baggage handling system ($9.3 million).[31] But McCarran's passenger volume quickly recovered after the 9/11 attacks; people still wanted to vacation in Las Vegas because of its themed mega-resorts with their affordable rooms, slot machines, entertainment, five-star restaurants, and other amenities. As more people came to Las Vegas, their numbers set new records. In 2002, 35,009,011 passengers passed through McCarran's gates. In 2005, that number reached 44,267,262.[32]

Though airport expansion had been postponed, with this passenger volume growth, Walker and his planning staff realized that further expansion was imminent, and they revised the plans in 2005 to accommodate a projected 55 million passengers, the airport's maximum capacity. They began looking at areas where the airport could expand. With houses and apartment buildings on the airport's periphery, airport officials offered more than 440 families equitable relocation to make way for expansion. The airport also offered to build a 22-acre public park in an adjoining neighborhood.[33] The master plan included two new terminals, bringing the total to four terminals. Terminal 3, an $800 million facility that would serve international airlines, was scheduled to open in 2007. A road expansion and access program would allow traffic to drive on Russell Road directly to the airport and would expand a tunnel underneath the runways that connected Interstate 215 with the airport. McCarran officials selected an 80-acre nearby site for consolidation of all eleven car rental companies. These road improvement plans and the rental car relocation would cost $1.4 billion.[34] The airport expansion program also included $5 million for a new air traffic control tower and $9 million for a new radar facility.[35] Though Walker and his staff were always prepared to deal with the economic volatility of the air travel industry, they did not anticipate the problems that would be generated by a sharp recession.

The airport had to prepare for US Airways' cutback in its number of daily round-trip flights to McCarran from 128 to 64 in February 2009. According to Andrew Nocella, US Airways senior vice president of marketing and planning, "Las Vegas has always been a low-fare leisure market but now the fares are considerably lower because of falling demand. When you take that and combine it with high fuel prices, Las Vegas has become extremely unprofitable for US Airways and would remain unprofitable indefinitely at its current size."[36] Airline analyst Mike Boyd saw it as a blow to Las Vegas, but more so to US Airways: "US Airways dropped those flights because they couldn't make any money on them. But I don't see it as a death blow for Las Vegas."[37]

Statistics clearly show that from 1998 to 2007 the volume of commercial airline passengers steadily increased, despite the September 11 attacks, and in 2008 and 2009 remained above 40 million passengers. Even though the city was in the grip of depressed economic conditions, airport officials continued to revise their outlook, basing their plans on the results of multimillion-dollar contractor studies projecting that the airport would arrive at maximum capacity by 2011 instead of 2012. Therefore, it was imperative to think about additional expansion at McCarran or to build a new airport. As columnist Tony Cook pointed out, "The problem is McCarran is expected to reach capacity by 2011 or 2012. And because it is not in the middle of the desert anymore, the airport's growth is limited by surrounding development."[38]

Passenger volume had grown steadily since 1948 when 35,106 passengers arrived at McCarran Field. In 1963 passenger volume reached 1.5 million. In 1996 more than 33 million passengers came to McCarran International Airport, and in 2002 McCarran became the seventh-busiest airport in the United States and the sixteenth busiest in the world, as measured by passenger traffic.[39] In 2007 it became the sixth busiest in the United States and fifteenth in the world. The reasons for this growth included not only the steadily increasing number of passengers but also the implementation of cutting-edge technology and enhanced amenities, prompting the local *Las Vegas Sun* newspaper to proclaim: "Besides building and maintaining the facility to accommodate the phenomenal growth in air traffic, McCarran has set the global standard for airport management and is known as [a leader] in technology and passenger amenities."[40] While there is little doubt that the national recession had some impact on tourism spending, people still came to Las Vegas to stay at the mega-resorts, to gamble, and to be entertained. McCarran Airport also continued to expand.

In 2007 the Federal Aviation Administration completed a study titled "Capacity Needs in the National Airspace System," which concluded that Las Vegas, like Chicago and San Diego, needed airfield, terminal, and roadway expansion. The report stated that McCarran could expect airport expansion through 2025, but Randall Walker claimed that given the growing number of passengers coming to McCarran each year, the airport likely would reach maximum capacity before that date.[41] He therefore pushed forward with plans to finish construction of the $770 million Terminal 3 and began an environmental study of the new airport in Ivanpah, scheduled to open in 2017 to handle 16 million more passengers.[42]

Despite the collapse of the national economy in 2008 and the consequent devastating impact on the Las Vegas economy, passenger volume at

McCarran Airport remained above 43 million, high enough to warrant further airport expansion. This included widening Russell Road, opening the fourth wing of Concourse D, which added nine more gates, jet bridges to enable more efficient and convenient passageways so that travelers catching connecting flights would not have to leave secure areas, retail space, and resurfacing of the tarmac. The expansion was vital not only to accommodate the increasing passenger volume but also to help generate annual revenues exceeding $500 million and to sustain the airport's direct and indirect economic impact on Nevada through fees, taxes, and the amount of money spent by travelers, which altogether amounted to $30 billion.[43]

Another important but controversial measure that McCarran operators implemented to reduce costs was allowing jets to make right turns as well as the accustomed left turns over residential areas. Turns in both directions minimized delays in air traffic flow, speeding up takeoffs and landings and allowing for more flights with more incoming passengers. Wealthy home owners in the right-turn area complained vociferously about the noise and the jet fuel smell polluting their peaceful neighborhoods, and they pressured the mayor and the city council to investigate violations of their home-owner rights. Las Vegas mayor Oscar Goodman expressed concern about the safety of flights over heavily populated residential areas. Middle-class residents in the left-turn area responded with appreciation that the arrogant, wealthy residents on Spanish Trail and in other upscale locations would have to endure jet noise.

Alan Feldman, CEO of the MGM Mirage, Nevada's largest hotel enterprise, which operated ten mega-resorts on the Strip, including the $9.2 billion City-Center, gave the right turn his firm approval. Needing to keep his hotel rooms fully occupied, he publicly criticized the complaining home owners: "A couple dozen residents are drumming up a dust storm at council meetings and the council is responding for purely political reasons."[44] With enough support from the airlines, the airport, the left-turn residents, and the hotel resorts, the city council voted unanimously to approve the right turn, which brought $281.3 million in cost savings to the airport with the arrival of 375,000 more passengers.[45] More resorts also appeared along Las Vegas Boulevard.

A Las Vegas Convention and Visitors Authority study showed that the portion of city visitors making $100,000 or more per year had jumped from 10 percent in 2003 to 24 percent in 2007.[46] This trend of both high passenger volume and increased numbers of high-end travelers caught the eye of wealthy mega-resort operators Steve Wynn, Sheldon Adelson, and others urging them to build bigger and better, not only for the masses but for those who had the money to fly, to stay, and to spend. As *Las Vegas Sun* journalist Jeff Simpson put it, "There is no denying that Las Vegas resorts are symbiotically linked to the airlines that bring in almost half of the city's visitors. But recent trends make clear that the city's dependence is about to get stronger. . . . The two newest Strip's [*sic*] resorts, Palazzo and Wynn Las Vegas, and resorts under construction including Encore, CityCenter, Fontainebleau, and Echelon are the kind of places less likely to attract drive-in customers."[47] As Las Vegas embraced the idea of even bigger and better, it was the airlines that made it possible.

Steve Wynn, especially, raised the bar in terms of sophistication when he built the two most luxurious mega-resorts on the Strip, the Wynn Las Vegas and the Encore. University of Nevada, Las Vegas public administration professor Bill Thompson commented that Wynn was in the forefront of Las Vegas's change toward focusing on richer, big-spending visitors and gamblers: "He sets the standard and others catch up to him. He understands these high rollers better than anyone." Thompson added, "With all suites and bigger rooms, this [Encore] will probably be where Wynn keeps some of his best casino guests."[48] Wynn built his posh resorts not for tourists but for his guests, according to Thompson. Wynn's other beautiful resorts on the Strip were wonderful attractions to him, Thompson continued. "But there is no franchise in the tourist attraction. There is a franchise in a guest and the guest is something that happens inside the building usually between the staff, the people of the building, and the building itself. . . . The audience isn't the sidewalk. The audience is the hotel. . . . You have to go inside. . . . And you are in a world of your own."[49] The world that Wynn created for his guests was exquisite.

His $2.7 billion super mega-resort Encore opened in October 2008, sitting on a 20-acre parcel of land once occupied by the famous Desert Inn resort. It contained 5,000 hotel rooms, 2,000 of which were luxury suites. The super mega-resort had several world-renowned, chef-designed and -operated restaurants, a massive convention center and meeting auditorium, high-end retail stores, a spa and salon, and entertainment venues. All suites were designed for higher-paying customers, with rates ranging from $284 to $2,000 per night.[50] A spectacular concert hall had seating for 3,000 with the capability to be converted into a giant ballroom suitable for dancing and conventions. According to Richard Branson, British billionaire and Virgin Airlines owner, "There is nobody in the world who creates such entertaining and beautiful casinos as Steve Wynn. Every other casino must be nervous. He has lifted the bar dramatically."[51]

In a keynote address at the International Gaming Business Exposition, billionaire and mega-resort mogul Sheldon Adelson admonished members that Las Vegas needed to improve the quality of its mega-resorts to attract a higher class of people, who he believed would spend more time and money if resort executives built properties with more luxury and amenities. He said, "Undifferentiated product additions to the same old rooms, $1.99 buffets, and casino lounges wrapped in a thematic façade do not constitute new thinking. They embody the worn-out assumptions which may have contributed to the recent slowdown in growth. . . . The Bellagio truly adds value to the Las Vegas Strip and the attractiveness of the city as a destination resort, not Circus Circus, the Aladdin, and Stratosphere, companies that built the same old products."[52]

But what Adelson did not mention in his speech was how his upscale guests got to Las Vegas. In 1998, more than 11 percent of the people who came to the city arrived by corporate or charter plane.[53] While existing mega-resorts expanded and new ones were built, many wealthy people continued to arrive in Las Vegas by first-class tickets on commercial airlines or on private jets. This was the reinvention of Las Vegas: more glitz, glamour, private jets, suites, and "whales" (big spenders) all in one location. And Wynn and Adelson helped facilitate the city's newest image.

The Palazzo, a $1.8 billion world-class luxury hotel casino and resort opened on January 17, 2008. It consisted of a fifty-story luxury hotel tower with 3,068 rooms, 375 concierge-level suites, and six villas of up to 11,000 square feet each. It also contained a 105,000-square-foot casino with 1,900 slot machines and 80 table games. The 250,000-square-foot pool deck connected with the Venetian's pool deck. The Palazzo's pool deck also housed an outdoor restaurant and two private villas. In February, a 270-unit condo tower was built, in addition to a 450,000-square-foot shopping mall, dining, and entertainment complex, with 80 high- and mid-tier retailers, all connected to the existing Canal shops at the Venetian. The property also had 450,000 square feet of meeting and conference space connected to the Sands Convention Center. Visitors to the Palazzo had access to the massive 4,000-space underground parking garage that led directly to the casino. This mega-resort catered to high-rolling gamblers, offering them high-class suites at a price of $25,000 per night, as well as private gambling rooms and personal servants. Upon completion, the combined Palazzo, Venetian, and Sands

Convention and Exposition Center, all Adelson properties, became the largest resort and hotel complex in the world, with 7,074 hotel rooms and suites.[54]

The popularity of Wynn's and Adelson's new luxury mega-resorts with the continuous influx of many tourists influenced the other Strip resort owners to upgrade and expand their properties. Caesars Palace built a $475 million, 900-room tower, a separate 665-room tower with an outdoor café, a wedding venue, and a 240,000-square-foot convention center, all at a cost of $1 billion. With this addition, the property had more than 300,000 square feet of available convention space, more than 4,000 rooms, and a gambler database exceeding 10 million clients.[55] The Bellagio built a $375 million, 925-room tower with a spa, 60,000 square feet of space for meetings, and 5,000 square feet of space for retail and restaurants. The Mandalay Bay added a $235 million, 1.8-million-square-foot convention center that contained a 100,000-square-foot ballroom and a 50,000-square-foot junior ballroom.[56] Planet Hollywood opened its $1.2 billion twin towers with 1,228 time-share condominiums. The Hard Rock Hotel added 875 more rooms to its property at a cost of $760 million.[57]

The new mega-resorts and other expanded resorts were easily outdone in size by the MGM-Mirage CityCenter project, the most ambitious in the world. This 76-acre metropolis in the heart of the Strip, which cost $9.2 billion to build, consisted of 18 million square feet of vertical development, a mixed-use cosmopolitan center of hotels, luxury condominiums, and shopping, all within an urban setting. Included was a skyline of two 400-room boutique hotels, one 4,000-room hotel and casino, four towers of 2,500 residential units, and 55,000 square feet of high-end dining and entertainment space. The tallest buildings were 65 to 70 stories in height, and the property also included a convention center. Visitors could gamble, shop in world-class retail stores like Louis Vuitton, Hermès, Prada, Christian Dior, Bulgari, Van Cleef & Arpels, and Tiffany, and dine at Beso, Mastro's Ocean Club, and two new Wolfgang Puck restaurants. They could also live in and promenade about the self-contained property without ever leaving it. CityCenter was the first on the Strip to combine private residences with hotels and casinos. Public squares, hidden parking structures, covered passageways, and a boulevard were all incorporated in the center.[58] These palatial tourist attractions drew enormous crowds of visitors from national and international cities who flew to Las Vegas on more than thirty airlines to experience the simulated feeling of living the opulent, pampered, wealthy lifestyle by shopping in world-class stores and enjoying the countless other amenities. The airlines, the airport, and the casino-resorts continued to work in a symbiotic fashion to enhance Las Vegas's position as a world-class tourist destination.

Though building the Palazzo, the Encore, and CityCenter added more than 45,000 rooms to the Strip and created 278,000 new jobs, the onset of the national recession in 2008 brought all construction of new resorts to a grinding halt. The downturn left resort contractors and owners with unfinished properties, tourists with less money to spend, and workers with the threat of massive layoffs.

The recession had especially harsh repercussions in Las Vegas. Collapse of the U.S. banking system, a steep decline in the economy, a sharp plunge in home values, and an explosive increase in the number of home foreclosures left Las Vegas in an economic predicament the like of which the city had not experienced since the Union Pacific railroad strike in 1922. "We are in a deep economic recession, bordering on depression," said former archivist and state historian Guy Rocha. "People are hurting and they are hurting badly."[59] Unemployment reached 14.2 percent with the loss of an additional 140,900 jobs. Las Vegas had more home foreclosures than any other large city in the nation, 28,000 residents fled the city, and the Strip was left with many unfinished construction sites.[60]

Wynn Resorts reported a loss of $159.6 million in the fourth quarter, compared to a profit of $65.5 million in the same quarter of the previous year. A *Las Vegas Sun* editorial stated: "Gaming companies are suffering from an oversupply of hotel rooms and excessive debt taken on during the boom years [2002–2007]. As gaming companies have cut jobs in response to the recession, the laid-off workers have had difficulty finding other work because of the lack of non-gaming job opportunities."[61]

The impact was made worse when tourists who did come to the city spent less money. *Las Vegas Sun* journalist Liz Benston observed: "Hotels are filling rooms with penny-pinching tourists in place of the expense account–wielding business travelers who flocked here before the recession."[62] This was an ominous sign for the mega-resorts, which depended not only on high visitor volume but also on generous visitor spending. Resort executives had overbuilt in response to the 2002–2007 boom in air travel and tourism. They had borrowed billions of dollars from Wall Street banks to expand existing properties and build even larger, more expensive resorts. When the banks failed in 2008, the mega-resorts were left with giant debts and needed a strong source of steady revenue to keep them afloat. Declines in tourist traffic magnified their problems. Mega-resort tycoon Steve Wynn noted the obvious: "People who lose their jobs can't go and spend money. People who have money when things get widespread get careful and don't spend money."[63] Serious measures had to be taken to bring visitors back to Las Vegas, even if it meant substantially reducing room rates at the debt-ridden resorts. Rooms normally priced at $300 or higher per night were soon reduced by half.

According to a quarterly report by Brookings Mountain West—a UNLV program that partners with the Brookings Institution think tank in Washington, D.C.—focusing on economic trends in the Intermountain West, from March 2009 to March 2010 Las Vegas had the sharpest increase in unemployment of all the nation's hundred largest metropolitan areas.[64] A question arose: Why is Las Vegas, a city noted for its rapid recovery from previous recessions, in so much worse shape than most other cities? Mark Muro, coauthor of the report, attributed the sluggish rebound to the city's dependence on tourism and real estate, both of which rely heavily on consumer spending: "Many consumers simply cannot afford to spend the amount of money they once did because they are under water in their mortgages or drowning in debt much more so than in prior recessions. Others are unwilling to spend because they are worried about losing their jobs."[65] John Restrepo, a Las Vegas economic analyst, echoed Muro's observations, saying that the Las Vegas economy is not particularly diversified, being heavily dependent on consumer spending and consumer confidence.[66] Terry Jicinsky, senior vice president of marketing for the Las Vegas Convention and Visitors Authority (LVCVA), noting a 10 percent decline in Las Vegas visitor volume in 2009, even expressed surprise at the staggering impact of the recession: "Because our growth cycle has been going on for twenty years, for many people, including myself, that's a career. That is the entire length of your experience. We have casino executives that started working in their 20s and 30s that are now in their 40s and 50s, where all they knew was double-digit growth year after year after year."[67]

The recession also dealt a heavy economic blow to an already ailing airline industry. With U.S. airlines overburdened by their own problems of enormous debt, too much competition, high fuel prices, and declining passenger numbers, it was up to the casino-resorts and the airport to find other means to take up the slack. US Airways drastically cut its number of flights to Las Vegas, and Allegiant Airlines pared down its flight schedule as well, which prompted an emergency meeting on June 20, 2008, attended by McCarran

Airport director Randall Walker, LVCVA vice president of marketing Terry Jicinsky, Allegiant Airlines CEO Maurice Gallagher, and US Airways CEO Doug Parker, to discuss ways McCarran could persuade Allegiant and US Airways to minimize their cutbacks. The situation also prompted the mega-resorts and the airport to reach out to international airlines to bring in global travelers who had the money to fly, could stay longer, and would spend more money. According to Jeff Voyles, a casino management professor at UNLV, the international travel market "was a great untapped market."[68]

Tourism boosters from the LVCVA and officials from McCarran traveled abroad to attend conferences with airline route planners to attract more direct and nonstop international flights. Developing services from existing markets and finding new markets were the goals. Las Vegas needed guests to fill its hotel rooms, but it also needed to be competitive with other domestic and global destinations. The value of routes conferences was the opportunity they provided for networking with many airlines from different countries.

Usually the major casinos do their marketing in foreign countries through their own long-established business offices instead of through mass marketing. During the recession, Harrah's Resorts, with the largest list of customers in the casino industry, enlisted Discover the World Marketing, 83 offices in 55 countries, to sell the seven major Harrah's properties on the Strip to travel agents, tour operators, and business groups in foreign countries. A Discover specialty was gathering travelers for foreign holidays not celebrated in the United States. MGM Mirage, a Harrah's competitor, connected directly with foreign travel agents and tour operators in addition to using its casino marketing offices.[69]

Historically, recruiting foreign tourists to Las Vegas was difficult because of expenses, visa-processing problems, and security demands. But good package deals made the trouble worth the effort. Las Vegas offered reasonably priced hotel rooms, one-stop airline services, and other amenities to foreign customers, which were very attractive. Though struggling domestic airlines cut many routes to and from Las Vegas, international air service increased in 2009 with additional flights from Canada and other countries because of the package deals. "What Las Vegas needs even more than incremental flights is more aggressive marketing to foreign tourists who may not perceive Las Vegas as a value," said Mike Boyd, an independent airline consultant.[70] Part of this effort included finding new ways to make international travel easier for all airlines.

On March 30, 2008, the United States signed an open-skies agreement with the European Union that went into effect to increase air traffic in the transatlantic market by easing restrictions dictating where United States and European air carriers could land. Since 1946, regulations and restrictions had governed who could fly where and when in the transatlantic airspace. The British government especially supported this policy because it feared that U.S. airlines would dominate the airspace and take away business from its airlines. To get authorization to fly through European airspace and land at European airports, the United States had to establish bilateral agreements with individual countries. By opening the transatlantic market through an open-skies agreement, European and U.S. airlines would also stand to make more profits by adding more international flights and attracting more paying passengers. Airports on both continents would profit through more airlines' paying takeoff and landing fees, renting ticket counter space, and renting jetways and through more passengers' spending money at airport concessions.

The open-skies agreement also meant more money for local communities through the creation of 80,000 jobs and 26 million more tourists over five years.[71] According to statistical data from the International Air Transport Association, in 2009 transatlantic air traffic increased 11 percent.[72] Besides the agreement with the European Union, the United States also signed bilateral agreements with the Philippines and ten other Southeast Asia countries, Australia, Chile, and New Zealand. Jeff Shane, a Washington, D.C., attorney who worked for the State Department and the Department of Transportation, credits airports for stimulating government thought and interest in bringing more international airlines to the United States and having more United States airlines serve other countries: "Until the airport operators got into the fray in Washington, which I date to the late 1980s, we really weren't able to make sensible progress in expanding markets, especially in bringing more foreign carrier service to the U.S."[73] Of course, airports, including McCarran International, now had to prepare themselves to find slots for 60 percent of the world's air traffic.

In May 2010, XL Airways France made its inaugural nonstop direct flight from Charles de Gaulle Airport in Paris, arriving at 6:40 P.M. at McCarran International Airport. According to Randall Walker, "Based on XL Airways current schedule, the airline could bring in 10,000 visitors to Las Vegas this summer, and that is great news for Clark County and the community as a whole."[74] The 2010 visitors profile study showed that these visitors brought $9.7 million in revenue to the city. XL Airways France will operate nonstop service to Las Vegas from Paris through September 23 on Thursdays and

Sundays using an Airbus A-330 with seating for 364 passengers. International traffic has been good for McCarran, up more than 15 percent from 2009. "We are very pleased to welcome first ever non-stop flights from Las Vegas to France," said Cathy Tull, LVCVA senior vice president of marketing. "France is a key source of overseas visitors to Las Vegas and this partnership with XL Airways broadens our accessibility to a market that has shown 19% growth in the last two years."[75]

In 2007, the Brookings Institution, which studies urban growth and design across the nation, declared Las Vegas a model city. With affordable housing, jobs, decent weather, and proximity to shops, restaurants, schools, the airport, and the casino resorts, Las Vegas was an ideal twenty-first-century city. According to a U.S. Department of Commerce study, from 2001 to 2006 Las Vegas experienced a 58 percent increase in personal income, compared to 42 percent in Phoenix and 23 percent in Denver.[76] Former Las Vegas mayor and city council member Jan Jones declared Las Vegas "one of the last cities in the world where true entrepreneurial spirit can flourish. The giant owners of this big destination are visionaries. They're competitive, fearless, and just as much gamblers as the guests they entertain."[77] In 2007, at the World Leadership Awards in London, Las Vegas was named American City of the Year, and the city's sustainability efforts for transportation and alternative fuels were specifically cited.[78] But with the devastating effects of the 2008 recession, the overarching question became this: How will Las Vegas pull out of this economic downturn that is affecting the entire metropolitan area?

Rory Reid, Clark County Commission chairman and a contender for the governor's race (and also the son of U.S. Senate majority leader Harry Reid), held that the only way Las Vegas, and more broadly Nevada, would survive the recession would be through the creation of more jobs and diversification of the economy. Reid contended that the state could no longer survive on tourism and gambling revenues alone and needed to bring other businesses to Nevada, businesses like those in modern technology and renewable energy. "I don't think anybody believes the gaming industry will take us to the promised land again," Reid said. "In our history that has been the prevalent view. There is urgency in the air. This is a unique opportunity to do the things we have always said we were going to do. We have to do it now. This is the moment."[79] But what Reid implied was that gambling and tourism were still important to the city's economy and that the airlines continued to play a vital role by bringing tourists and gamblers to Las Vegas.

An article by *Las Vegas Sun* journalist Patrick Coolican compared Las

Vegas to Rust Belt cities that also depend on a single economy—Detroit on automobiles, Pittsburgh on steel, and Las Vegas on gambling and tourism. After posing the question of how cities achieve goals of diversification and progress, Coolican wrote: "The answer is simple. You have to produce something fresh and new such as renewable energy technology that will blow the doors off the market place, or a resort so incredible—like the Mirage in 1989—the tourists just have to see it. . . . You have to innovate. Where does the innovation come from? In part, from sheer entrepreneurialism."[80] But it also comes from airlines' continuing to deliver millions of tourists and gamblers annually to Las Vegas's mega-resorts.

Las Vegas mayor Oscar Goodman strongly exercised the entrepreneurial spirit when he convinced the city council to draft plans for redeveloping the downtown business district. Included in the plans were a high-rise tower for the International Jewelry Center with a 165,000-square-foot retail center, promenade, banking facilities, and restaurants; the building and landscaping of Union Park—a 61-acre plot for office, hotel, and residential space; construction of the Cleveland Clinic Lou Ruvo Center for Brain Health, designed by world-renowned architect Frank Gehry; and the Smith Center for the Performing Arts, a $475 million, four-theater complex.[81]

The Jewelry Center chose to relocate to Las Vegas because the city has been one of the fastest-growing metropolitan areas in the United States and is one of the most visited international cities in the world, attributes that make it a perfect place for global jewelry manufacturers and artisans to live and conduct business. The Lou Ruvo Center for Brain Health, operated by the famous Cleveland Clinic, a multispecialty medical center in Cleveland, Ohio, was planned to become the national resource for the most current research and scientific information in the treatment of Alzheimer's disease. According to promotional materials from the Smith Center for the Performing Arts, "Las Vegas is poised to make the leap from popular tourist destination to one of the nation's leading cosmopolitan hubs. Upon completion, the Smith Center will place Las Vegas on the world stage for performing arts, attracting world-class artistry, diverse productions, and a highly-skilled workforce."[82]

Globalizing Las Vegas with these world-class facilities in conjunction with the opening of CityCenter, the Echelon, and the Fontainebleau mega-resorts and the expansion of McCarran International Airport, will help provide a route by which the city can recover from the recession and better diversify its economy. Though Las Vegas is becoming a high-class, highly cultured metropolis comparable to Los Angeles and New York, it still sits in the Mojave Desert, and depends heavily upon the airlines to bring in business, including international travelers.

"In today's airline business, if you are not global you are not a player," said Clive Irving, senior consulting editor of *Condé Nast Traveler* magazine.[83] The recent merger of United Airlines with Continental and the 2008 merger of Delta with Northwest Airlines, now the two largest air carriers in the world, and major airlines serving Las Vegas, have better connected Las Vegas with the rest of the world. By combining their domestic networks with international routes, the airlines offered more choices for leisure and business travelers—more destinations, a larger selection of flight times, and more services. Of course, they are in strong competition with Lufthansa, Air France/KLM, Singapore Airlines, and Emirates, all of them airlines with long-established routes and clientele who pay top dollar for premium service.

Las Vegas has its eye on China, a giant international market with enormous numbers of travelers flying all over the globe, with U.S. destinations in high demand. According to Irving, "Given that international traffic is usually more profitable than domestic, they [the airlines] will be fine-tuning routes realigning their Pacific hubs to maximize their ability to tap into that roaring wave of Chinese travelers, many of whom will be heading for the US. And once they board a US carrier, they will be locked into that carrier's domestic network."[84] By tapping into the China market, Las Vegas will attract more customers, increase revenue from tourism and gambling, and give the city even greater international presence.

Part of attracting international travelers to a world-class destination is offering them facilities with amenities, services, entertainment, fine dining, and recreational activities, all at a reasonable price. The other part is providing comfortable travel accommodations. For international airlines serving Las Vegas, this means using modern, state-of-the-art passenger planes such as the Boeing 777, which British Airways flies daily from London Heathrow to McCarran International Airport, and soon the new, much anticipated Boeing 787 Dreamliner.

This new passenger jet has seating for 250 passengers, uses minimal-energy lighting, has an energy-efficient galley, and more notably, is made of lighter, composite materials, making it the most aerodynamic and fuel-efficient jet ever. Despite the two-year production delay because of design flaws, when the Dreamliner comes into service in the very near future, the airline industry will experience nothing short of another revolution in air travel. Not only can this plane carry more passengers than most of its competitors, but it uses 20 percent less fuel than the wide-bodied 767 and can comfortably fly more than 8,500 miles without refueling. The benefits of the 787's light airframe and fuel-efficient engines will allow airlines that add it to their fleets to save millions of dollars.[85]

Conclusion

Commercial air travel is the lifeblood of Las Vegas.

DUANE BUSCH

*A*t 8:30 P.M., on October 25, 2009, British Airways Flight 275 touched down at McCarran International Airport after a 10-hour, 50-minute inaugural flight from London's Heathrow International Airport. Among the 217 paying passengers on board was British Airways CEO Willie Walsh, making his first trip to southern Nevada and escorted by Las Vegas mayor Oscar Goodman, Rossi Ralenkotter, CEO and president of the Las Vegas Convention and Visitors Authority, and two other LVCVA executives.[1]

For the special occasion, British Airways chose one of its most luxurious jumbo jets, the Boeing 777-200 with First Class, Club World (business class), World Traveler Plus (premium economy class), and World Traveler (economy class) services. As the jumbo jet taxied to the international terminal, a waiting McCarran fire brigade spouted a giant water arch under which the plane passed, a grand welcome reserved for maiden flights. After deplaning and going through customs, passengers were given a special greeting by Clark County Department of Aviation director Randall Walker, representatives from the luxurious Wynn Las Vegas resort where CEO Walsh would be a guest of honor, members of the news media, and two beautiful Las Vegas showgirls. Mayor Goodman's words to the assembled crowd summed up the special nature of the event: "This is a great day for Las Vegas and a great day for London."[2]

For nearly a decade, McCarran International Airport officials and the LVCVA had tried unsuccessfully to convince British Airways that Las Vegas had much to offer its clientele. With Virgin Atlantic Airlines making daily nonstop trips since 2006 from Gatwick International Airport, London's second busiest, and British Midland International doing long-haul flights from

Manchester, the United Kingdom had become the primary source of over-seas travelers to Las Vegas, with nearly 400,000 visitors in 2008 alone. So it made sense to form a partnership with the largest of the United Kingdom's air carriers. British Airways annually flew 36 million travelers to 143 world-wide destinations in 69 countries, was based at Heathrow International Airport, the largest and busiest of London's six airports, and would give Las Vegas the advantage of an extensive global network from which to draw thousands more international travelers.[3]

British Airways indicated that it was more than satisfied with all that the resort city had to offer when it confirmed the Las Vegas route with the assign-ment of its flagship Boeing 777, designated for only direct daily flights. Other international carriers had begun operating at McCarran on a trial basis with a few flights per week, but British Airways became the first regularly sched-uled overseas airline to begin daily operations, a vote of confidence in the city's ability to draw worldwide travelers.

Advance bookings from London to Las Vegas were sold out with pas-sengers who paid $663.10 for a round-trip ticket, prompting CEO Walsh to remark that the Las Vegas route was the best-performing new route he had ever seen, and that he would speak with "great passion" about the resort city.[4] The LVCVA assured him that with its strong marketing connections in many European countries, it would in turn include British Airways in its advertis-ing. Walsh was impressed with Las Vegas as a world-class travel destination with its luxurious internationally themed mega-resorts that were so attrac-tive to global travelers. He pledged that British Airways would provide pack-age deals assuring its travelers affordable airfare, deluxe hotel accommo-dations, fine international cuisine, and high-end entertainment. McCarran offered British Airways cheap airport fees, which would help lower operating costs, and impressed the company with the rapid progress being made on the construction of Terminal 3, which would be equipped with cutting-edge systems designed to most efficiently process thousands of international pas-sengers, minimizing delays.[5]

McCarran International Airport was ready for the assigned Boeing 777 jumbo jet with its 272 passenger seats, meals prepared by world-class chefs, and entertainment systems including movies, television programs, music, and outlets for personal computers.[6] The carrier was scheduled to leave Heathrow daily at 3:35 P.M. and arrive in Las Vegas the next evening at 7:25 P.M., with return Flight 274 leaving Las Vegas daily at 9:20 P.M. and arriving in London the next day at 2:05 P.M. *Las Vegas Sun* journalist Rich Velotta, among the welcoming crowd at the gate, said of the special event: "Everything is good for Las Vegas. It has nonstop round trips to Heathrow and Gatwick. It has great connections to the rest of Europe, the Middle East, Africa, and Asia. It has world-renowned companies to partner with. It couldn't have happened at a better time when the city [in a time of deep national recession] could use an economic lift," hopefully returning to the 2002–2007 years of the highest air traveler and visitor volumes in the city's history.[7]

Commercial air travel enabled Las Vegas to become a model twenty-first-century American city and an internationally famous tourist mecca. With passenger planes annually delivering more than 30 million air travelers and tourists from national and international points of origin to McCarran Airport and the luxurious mega-resorts on the Strip, Las Vegas joined Los Angeles, Phoenix, San Francisco, New York, and Chicago as cities that rose to prominence by connecting to a rapidly expanding commercial aviation industry. The passenger plane was especially important to Las Vegas because the town depended heavily on tourism as its primary source of revenue, and passenger planes provided the vehicles that gamblers and tourists needed to get to the desert resort city. Thus a symbiotic partnership developed among the airlines, the airport, the casino-resorts, and the government that grew steadily, with the last three developing a dependence on the first for business. But the airlines could not accomplish this partnership alone.

Government funding enabled the airline industry to thrive. Without Uncle Sam's financial assistance, the airline industry was too expensive for private financiers to sustain, and would have faced imminent collapse. This pattern was especially evident during the infant and adolescent years of the industry (the 1920s–1950s), and again in later years when the airlines continued their dependence on the federal government for subsidization in the form of loans for airplane leases, daily flight operations, and transportation of mail. Las Vegas, itself a town that had depended on federal government funding for its economic survival, eagerly embraced the new form of transportation that would bring in business. In addition, the city had the good fortune to be in close proximity to heavily populated Southern California, the birthplace and center of the nation's giant aerospace and aircraft industries, where air travel in the West originated and from which a hefty flow of tourists came to the southern Nevada desert for more than eight decades. But advancement in aircraft technology and changes to government regulatory policy of the airline industry brought substantial change to the country and Las Vegas during deregulation, when airlines became able to set their own fares and routes, and the air travel and tourism industry boomed.

Despite struggles with deep debt, poor management, labor issues, and high fuel costs, the airlines continued to be part of the growing air travel, gambling, and tourism industries in Las Vegas. Even though US Airways and Allegiant Airlines reduced their number of flights to Las Vegas, McCarran Airport still remained the seventh-busiest domestic airport, and the fifteenth-busiest international airport in the world, handling more than 1,100 flights per day and welcoming more than 40 million passengers per year. Those numbers were higher than they have been since 1980. For years, casino-resort executives, airport officials, and city officials have understood how essential the airlines have become to Las Vegas's sustenance and future growth, and thus they have made the airlines and McCarran Airport an integral part of future urban planning and development.

The twenty-first century, however, is bringing new and important challenges to the airline industry through major airline mergers, reduced service to various locations, which not only means fewer flights, but limited time schedules, and increased fees for baggage, seats, and in-flight services. The airlines continue to leave an unfortunate carbon footprint of contamination of the skies, continuing dependence on fossil fuels, and invasive noise pollution at heavily congested airports. Much work remains to be done toward a global open-skies agreement allowing the world's airlines to fly through each other's airspace and do business with each other's markets. These problems raise questions that only the airlines, the airport, and the city of Las Vegas can resolve.

Notes

▶ *Introduction*

1. Las Vegas McCarran International Airport News Release, "Terminal 3 More than 50% Complete," January 2010, 12, http://www.mccarran.com.

2. Hawley, *The New Deal and the Problem of Monopoly,* 240.

CHAPTER ONE ▶ *The Airlines Come to Las Vegas*

1. Evensen, "Vegas Air History." Also see Harrington, "History of Aviation in Las Vegas Valley," 5.

2. Evensen, "Vegas Air History," 12.

3. Ibid. Also see Robert Griffith, former postmaster general, to Arthur F. Kelly, Delta Airlines vice president of sales, September 10, 1962, Western Airlines Collection, Delta Airlines Archive, Atlanta.

4. Quoted in Courtwright, *Sky as Frontier,* 59.

5. Bender and Altschul, *The Chosen Instrument,* 65.

6. *Clark County Review,* October 23, 1920, 1.

7. Ibid., October 9, 1920, 1.

8. Ibid., June 11, 1921, 1.

9. "Air Mail May Come This Way," ibid., February 12, 1921, 1. Also see "May Route Air Mail via Vegas," ibid., October 23, 1920, 1.

10. *Clark County Review,* March 19, 1921, 1.

11. Wright, *Desert Airways,* 5.

12. *Clark County Review,* March 19, 1926, 1.

13. Honorable W. W. Hawes, Second Assistant Postmaster General in Washington D.C., Summarization of Western Air Express, July 1, 1933, 1, in Western Airlines Collection, Delta Airlines Archive, Atlanta.

14. Davies, *Airlines of the United States Since 1914,* 43, 65. Also see Hawes, Summarization of Western Air Express, 1.

15. Solberg, *Conquest of the Skies,* 38. Also see Hawes, Summarization of Western Air Express, 2, 38; and Davies, *Airlines of the United States Since 1914,* 65.

16. Hawes, Summarization of Western Air Express, 2, 3.

17. Bilstein, *Flight in America,* 30–31.

18. Ibid.

19. Wilson and Handlin, *Herbert Hoover,* 113, 120.

20. Office of the Federal Register, *Public Papers of the Presidents of the United States: Herbert Hoover, 1929* (1974), 145. Also see Wilbur and Hyde, *The Hoover Policies,* 215, 216.

21. Solberg, *Conquest of the Skies,* 63. Also see Wilbur and Hyde, *The Hoover Policies,* 216–218; and *Public Papers of Presidents of the United States: Hoover, 1929,* 145.

22. Heppenheimer, *Turbulent Skies,* 14.

23. Roske, *Las Vegas,* 69. Also see "Plane Conveys Human Freight," *Salt Lake Tribune,* May 24, 1926, 1.

24. Embry, "Air Travel in the Southwest," 13.

25. *Southern California Rapid Transportation District Newsletter,* July 28, 1976, 5. Also see Solberg, *Conquest of the Skies,* 104.

26. Las Vegas Chamber of Commerce Minutes, January 4, 1927.

27. *Las Vegas Review-Journal,* June 28, 1964, 55.

28. *Clark County Review,* February 5, 1921, 1.

29. Ibid., December 30, 1921, 1.

30. Armstrong, Robinson, and Hoy, *History of Public Works in the United States,* 188.

31. Wright, *Desert Airways,* 5.

32. Robert Griffith, former postmaster general to Arthur F. Kelly, vice president of sales at Delta Airlines, September 10, 1962, Delta Airlines Collection, Atlanta.

33. Moehring, *Resort City in the Sunbelt,* 3–7.

34. Rothman, *Neon Metropolis,* 5.

35. Roske, *Las Vegas,* 77.

36. Moehring, *Resort City in the Sunbelt,* 18.

37. Roske, *Las Vegas,* 85. Also see Irv Owen in Russo, *The Outfit,* 286, 287. Also see Denton and Morris, *The Money and the Power,* 174.

38. Nevada State Assemblyman Phil Tobin, quoted in Land and Land, *A Short History of Las Vegas,* 84.

39. Russo, *The Outfit,* 286.

40. Harrington, "History of Aviation in the Las Vegas Valley," 4.

41. Hawes, Summarization of Western Air Express, 2. Also see Launius and Embry, "Fledgling Wings," 17.

42. *Chicago Herald and Examiner,* July 2, 1927, in *Flying Across America,* by Rust, 8.

43. Marcia Davenport, "Covered Wagon—1932," *Good Housekeeping,* October 1932, in *Flying Across America,* by Rust, 13.

44. Bilstein, *Flight in America,* 57.

45. Senator Hugo Black to Walter Folger Brown, January 27, 1934, Walter Folger Brown Papers, Ohio Historical Society, Columbus.

46. Postmaster General James A. Farley to Walter Folger Brown, January 19, 1934, ibid.

47. Walter Folger Brown to William Randolph Hearst, February 9, 1934, ibid. Also note that Brown sought Hearst's assistance to clear his name.

48. Walter Folger Brown to Senator Simeon D. Fess, February 10, 1934, ibid.

49. Solberg, *Conquest of the Skies,* 113.

50. Ibid.

51. Message from Senator Patrick McCarran to the National Aviation Forum, January 7, 1940, Senator Patrick McCarran Collection, Nevada Historical Society, Reno.

52. U.S. Senate Committee on Commerce hearing of S.3187, April 12, 1934, ibid. Also see *Washington Daily News,* April 27, 1934, 1; and *Washington Herald,* April 28, 1934, 5.

53. Statement from Senator McCarran, McCarran Collection.

54. Solberg, *Conquest of the Skies,* 145.

55. Wright, *Desert Airways,* 14.

56. Bilstein, *The Enterprise of Flight,* 42. Also see Solberg, *Conquest of the Skies,* 160.

57. Solberg, *Conquest of the Skies,* 166.

58. Bilstein, *Flight in America* 91.

59. Serling, *The Only Way to Fly,* 177.

60. Launius and Embry, "Fledgling Wings," 21.

61. *Las Vegas Review-Journal,* October 30, 1936, 1.

62. U.S. Government, *Report on the Works Program,* March 16, 1936, 2, 5, 31, in Embry, "Building the Infrastructure."

63. Hawley, *The New Deal and the Problem of Monopoly,* 243. Also see Biederman, *The United States Airline Industry,* xi.

64. Nevada Senator Patrick McCarran, Memorandum, January 9, 1940, McCarran Collection. Also see Hawley, *The New Deal and the Problem of Monopoly,* 243.

65. Nevada Senator Patrick McCarran Memorandum, January 11, 1940, McCarran Collection.

66. Message to the National Aviation Forum, February 7, 1940, ibid.

67. Nevada Senator Patrick McCarran, Speech to the National Aeronautics Association, January 12, 1940, ibid.

68. *Las Vegas Review-Journal,* November 14, 1939, 1.

69. Wright, *Desert Airways,* 16. Also see Moehring, *Resort City in the Sunbelt,* 32.

70. *Las Vegas Age,* February 7, 1941, 1, McCarran Collection.

71. Ibid., 13.

CHAPTER TWO ► *A Symbiotic Relationship Forms*

1. Kennedy, *The Rise and Fall of the Great Powers,* 455.

2. Solberg, *Conquest of the Skies,* 251. Also see Schwantes, *Going Places,* 261.

3. Clark County Department of Aviation, "McCarran 2000: Reflections of the Past," 18.

4. Davies, *Airlines of the United States Since 1914,* 289.

5. Schwantes, *Going Places,* 267.

6. Roske, *Las Vegas,* 91. Also see Moehring, *Resort City in the Sunbelt,* 37; and Moehring and Green, *Las Vegas,* 104.

7. Moehring, *Resort City in the Sunbelt,* 40.

8. Elliott, *The New Western Frontier,* 40, 43. Also see McCracken, *Las Vegas,* 53–54; and Kropp, *California "Vieja,"* 169.

9. Michael S. Green, *Online Nevada Encyclopedia,* January 1, 2009, 1, http://onlinenevada.org/; Moehring, *Resort City in the Sunbelt,* 45.

10. Moehring, *Resort City in the Sunbelt,* 45.

11. "Airport Gave Wings to Growth of Las Vegas," *Las Vegas Sun,* December 16, 2003, 1–4.

12. Schwantes, *Going Places,* 273.

13. Bilstein, *Flight in America,* 97.

14. Solberg, *Conquest of the Skies,* 333.

15. Courtwright, *Sky as Frontier,* 127.

16. Arthur Kelly, vice president of sales, Western Air Express, to the Chambers of Commerce in San Diego, Palm Springs, Phoenix, Las Vegas, and Los Angeles, March 3, 1952, in Delta Airlines Collection, Atlanta.

17. Petzinger, *Hard Landing,* 349, 377.

18. Grossman, *American Express,* 261.

19. Bilstein, *Flight in America,* 172, 176.

20. *Las Vegas Review-Journal,* January 3, 1950, 3.

21. Ibid.

22. Tyndall, "United Airlines in Las Vegas," 3.

23. Western Air Express advertisement, October 1956, Lied Library Special Collections, University of Nevada, Las Vegas. Also see *Las Vegas Review-Journal,* August 2, 1949, 5.

24. Moehring, *Resort City in the Sunbelt,* 32.

25. Ibid. Also see Churchill, "How to Build an Airport," 38; and Burnham, "In the Crockett Tradition," 28.

26. James V. Piersol, "International Air Bill Review Set Tomorrow," *Washington Post,* February 6, 1945, 3, McCarran Collection. Also see "Single U.S. World Airline Is Proposed," *San Francisco Chronicle,* December 1, 1945, 2, ibid.

27. McCarran Airport Dedication Program, December 19, 1948, ibid. Also see Senator McCarran's speech to the National Aeronautics Association in New Orleans, January 12, 1940, 22, ibid.

28. *Las Vegas Review-Journal,* August 25, 1960, 6. Also see Burnham, "In the Crockett Tradition," 28, 78.

29. McCarran Airport Dedication Program, December 19, 1948. Also see *Las Vegas Review-Journal,* December 19, 1948, B1; and Moehring, *Resort City in the Sunbelt,* 62.

30. Moehring, *Resort City in the Sunbelt,* 62. Also see *Las Vegas Sun,* June 11, 1998, E7.

31. McCarran Airport Dedication Program, December 19, 1948, McCarran Collection.

32. *Boulder City Journal,* December 23, 1948, B1.

33. *Las Vegas Review-Journal,* January 17, 1952, 3, and January 22, 1952, 4. Also see *Las Vegas Life,* June 1947, 14–15; and *Las Vegas Review-Journal,* February 19, 1953, 6.

34. *Las Vegas Review-Journal,* November 18, 1960, 3.

35. Ibid., March 14, 1957, 4. Also see Clark County Commission Minutes, August 15, 1957.

36. Lou Davis, *Flying,* May 1961, 29. Also see *Aviation Week and Space Technology,* April 9, 1962, 24.

37. *Las Vegas Review-Journal,* May 24, 1960, 1.

38. Skidmore, "Gaming Junkets in Nevada," 27. Also see Walters, "Study of Gambling Junkets."

39. Linn, *Big Julie of Las Vegas*, 3.

40. William J. Moore, interview by Elizabeth Harrington, Reno, 1981.

41. Parrish, "New Aviation Power Center," 15.

42. Torgerson, *Kerkorian*, 76.

43. Parrish, "New Aviation Power Center," 15. Also see Palermo, "Kirk Kerkorian," 163.

44. Stamos Jr., *Las Vegas Review Magazine*, 1.

45. Moehring, *Resort City in the Sunbelt*, 81.

46. Ibid., 7, 81.

47. Taylor, *Casino News*, 1.

48. Hotel advertisement from 1956, Lied Library Special Collections, University of Nevada, Las Vegas.

49. Richard Taylor, general manager, Hacienda Hotel, interview by Daniel Bubb, Las Vegas, April 26, 2000.

50. Stamos, *Las Vegas Review Magazine*, August 12 1979, 7; *Las Vegas Sun*, February 14, 1991, A32.

51. Reid and Demaris, *The Green Felt Jungle*, 50. For Bayley's ownership of the Hacienda and the New Frontier hotels, see 224, 228.

52. *Las Vegas Review-Journal*, May 5, 1961, 5.

53. Taylor interview.

54. *Los Angeles Herald Examiner*, July 21, 1962, A16.

55. Boyd Michael, chief pilot and director of pilot training at Hacienda Airlines, telephone interview by author, May 1, 2000.

56. *Las Vegas Review-Journal*, October 23, 1961, 2. Also see *Los Angeles Herald Examiner*, October 17, 1962, D1.

57. Paul Price, *Las Vegas Sun*, June 16, 1960, 4.

58. Denton and Morris, *The Money and the Power*, 128, 145.

59. Russo, *The Outfit*, 233.

60. Rothman, *Devil's Bargains*, 296.

61. Kaufman, "City Boosters, Las Vegas Style," 48.

62. John Findlay, in Elliott, *The New Western Frontier*, 63.

63. Rothman and Davis, *The Grit Beneath the Glitter*, 245.

64. Denton and Morris, *The Money and the Power*, 137–143.

65. *Las Vegas Review-Journal Sunday Edition*, December 5, 1954, 38.

66. *Las Vegas Review-Journal*, October 23, 1957, 2.

67. Clark County Commission Minutes, August 6, 1958.

68. *Las Vegas Review-Journal*, December 13, 1957, 4.

69. Clark County Commission Minutes, May 8, 1958, May 28, 1958, and May 6, 1959. Also see *Las Vegas Review-Journal*, February 25, 1960, 3.

70. Clark County Commission Minutes, May 27, 1958.

71. Ibid., June 30, 1959.

72. Clark County Department of Aviation, "McCarran 2000: Reflections of the Past," 22. Also see Moehring, *Resort City in the Sunbelt*, 132.

73. Clark County Department of Aviation, "McCarran 2000: Reflections of the Past," 22.

74. Clark County Commission Minutes, November 6, 1957, December 22, 1958.

75. *Las Vegas Review-Journal,* March 3, 1960, 2.

76. Ibid., February 25, 1960, 6.

77. Ibid., March 17, 1960, 2.

78. Bilstein, *Flight in America,* 233.

79. *Las Vegas Sun,* June 11, 1998, E7.

80. *Las Vegas Review-Journal,* March 3, 1960, 3.

81. Rothman, *Devil's Bargains,* 301–302.

CHAPTER THREE   ►   *Jets in the Consumer Age*

1. Solberg, *Conquest of the Skies,* 345.

2. Ibid.

3. Bilstein, *Flight in America,* 257.

4. Moehring, *Resort City in the Sunbelt,* 132.

5. *Las Vegas Review-Journal,* February 3, 1950, 3.

6. *Las Vegas Sun,* March 15, 1963, 18.

7. Heppenheimer, *Turbulent Skies,* 185.

8. Ibid.

9. Bilstein, *Flight in America,* 257.

10. Newman, "When Everybody Dined First Class."

11. Lukas, "On the Wings of Commerce," 4.

12. *Las Vegas Review-Journal,* February 25, 1960, 6.

13. Heppenheimer, *Turbulent Skies,* 186.

14. *Las Vegas Sun,* March 15, 1963, 17.

15. *Aviation Week and Space Technology,* March 14, 1966, 262–264.

16. *Las Vegas Review-Journal,* November 18, 1960, 24.

17. Memo to the Associated Press, January 25, 1962, Nevada Senator Alan Bible Collection, University of Nevada, Reno.

18. *Aviation Week and Space Technology,* September 10, 1962, 26.

19. "Delta Observes Fifteen Years of Service to Las Vegas," *Delta Air Lines News,* June 25, 1976, Delta Airlines Collection, Atlanta.

20. Statement from Nevada Senator Alan Bible in the Southern Transcontinental Service Case, Docket 7984, September 26, 1961, Nevada Senator Alan Bible Collection.

21. "Delta Observes Tenth Anniversary Here," *Delta Air Lines News,* July 1, 1971, Delta Airlines Collection.

22. *Las Vegas Sun,* March 15, 1963, 18.

23. "Delta Observes Fifteen Years of Service to Las Vegas."

24. *Las Vegas Review-Journal,* October 6, 1968, 9.

25. "TWA's Financing Proposal Appears to Be Discarded," *Wall Street Journal,* October 25, 1960, 24. Also see Ed Koch, "Hughes' Legacy Looms Large in LV," *Las Vegas Sun,* December 23, 2004, 3.

26. "Air West to Hughes," *Los Angeles Herald Examiner,* April 15, 1969, D7.

27. *Las Vegas Sun,* April 4, 1975, 8.

28. *Las Vegas Review-Journal,* May 7, 1974, 7, April 4, 1975, 8. Also see *Las Vegas Sun,* January 20, 1969, 16.

29. *Las Vegas Review-Journal,* May 8, 1974, 38.

30. Mary Manning, "Howard Hughes: A Revolutionary Recluse," *Las Vegas Sun,* May 15, 2008, 2.

31. Ibid.

32. Ibid.

33. Ibid.

34. Moehring, *Resort City in the Sunbelt,* 230.

35. Ibid., 119.

36. Petzinger, *Hard Landing,* 408.

37. *Public Papers of the Presidents of the United States: Harry S. Truman, 1945* (1961), 1144.

38. Ibid. Also see *Public Papers of the Presidents of the United States: Dwight D. Eisenhower, 1953* (1953), 483.

39. Armstrong, Robinson, and Hoy, *History of Public Works in the United States,* 197.

40. President John F. Kennedy to the Senate and House of Representatives, April 24, 1961, in *Public Papers of the Presidents of the United States: John F. Kennedy* (1961–1963), 315–316.

41. Schwantes, *Going Places,* 198. For the $75 million figure, see Kennedy's letter to the Senate and House of Representatives, April 24, 1961, *Public Papers,* 316.

42. Press release, March 23, 1961, Nevada Senator Howard Cannon Collection, Lied Library Special Collection, University of Nevada, Las Vegas.

43. Ibid. Also see *Las Vegas Review-Journal,* October 24, 1965, 14.

44. *Las Vegas Review-Journal,* April 11, 1976, 4.

45. Ibid., March 14, 1963, 3.

46. Evensen, "Vegas Air History," 12; *Las Vegas Review-Journal,* October 4, 1985, 12. Also see *Las Vegas Sun,* June 11, 1998, E8.

47. Nevada Senator Alan Bible to McCarran Airport Director Gordon Miles, February 20, 1963, in Senator Alan Bible Collection, University of Nevada, Reno.

48. *Las Vegas Review-Journal,* January 3, 1976, 17.

49. Ibid., April 11, 1976, 4.

50. *Las Vegas Sun,* June 11, 1998, E8.

51. Moehring, *Resort City in the Sunbelt,* 109.

52. Landrum and Brown Consultants, Master plan, II-2.

53. Landrum and Brown Consultants, Executive Summary, V-2, V-3, II-9, II-10.

54. TRA Consultants Executive Summary, October 1, 1979, 4, 5.

55. Ibid., 22.

56. Rothman, *Neon Metropolis,* 17, 18. Also see Russo, *The Outfit,* 461, 462.

57. Roske, *Las Vegas,* 114.

58. Ibid.

59. *Las Vegas Sun,* January 25, 2001, 2.

60. *Holiday* magazine, July 1961, in *The Money and the Power,* by Denton and Morris, 145.

61. Moehring, *Resort City in the Sunbelt,* 108.

62. *Las Vegas Review-Journal,* September 11, 1975, 1.

63. Pomeroy, *The American Far West in the 20th Century,* 194, 195.

64. *Las Vegas Review-Journal,* March 9, 1977, 21.

65. Ibid.

66. Bilstein, *Flight in America,* 285–286.

67. Solberg, *Conquest of the Skies,* 345, 406.

68. Ibid., 349.

69. Petzinger, *Hard Landing,* 18; Solberg, *Conquest of the Skies,* 348, 349.

70. *Las Vegas Sun,* March 5, 1960, 5. Also see *Las Vegas Review-Journal,* March 30, 1975, 1. Also see Clark County Department of Aviation, McCarran Airport passenger statistics for enplaned and deplaned passengers, 1969–1970, http://www.mccarran .com.

71. *Las Vegas Sun,* November 16, 1968, 9. Also see *Las Vegas Review-Journal,* March 7, 1977, 23.

CHAPTER FOUR ► *Airline Deregulation and the Mega-Resorts*

1. Clark County Department of Aviation, "McCarran 2000: Reflections of the Past," 48, 52, 60.

2. Duane Busch, TWA executive station manager, interview by author, January 7, 2001.

3. Susan Davis, Southwest Airlines marketing representative, interview by author, Las Vegas, January 4, 2001.

4. U.S. House Subcommittee on Aviation, 106th Congress, 1st hearing, October 20–21, 1999.

5. U.S. Senate Committee on Commerce, Science, and Transportation, *Antitrust Issues in the Airline Industry,* 106th Congress, 1st hearing, July 27, 2000.

6. United States General Accounting Office Report, February 23, 1977; *Public Papers of the Presidents of the United States: Jimmy Carter, 1977* (1977), 245.

7. *Jimmy Carter,* 245.

8. U.S. House Subcommittee on Aviation, 106th Congress, hearing, October 20–21, 1999.

9. Ibid.

10. U.S. House Subcommittee on Aviation, 104th Congress, *Domestic Air Service in the Wake of Airline Deregulation: Challenges Faced by Small Carriers,* 1st hearing, April 25, 1996.

11. U.S. Senate Committee on Commerce, Science, and Transportation, 98th Congress, *Oversight of Airline Deregulation,* 1st hearing, June 27–28, 1983.

12. Davis interview. Also see McCarran International Airport Newsletter, January 24, 1997, http://www.mccarran.com. Also see Clark County Department of Aviation News Release, January 19, 1997, January 19, 1998, January 19, 1999, January 19, 2000, January 19, 2001, http://www.mccarran.com.

13. Petzinger, *Hard Landing,* 29, 330. Also see Davis interview, January 4, 2001.

14. *Las Vegas Review-Journal,* November 14, 1998, D1.

15. Jennifer Myers, America West marketing manager, telephone interview by author, January 4, 2001.

16. Ibid.

17. Ibid.

18. *Los Angeles Herald,* January 26, 2001, 1.

19. *Airways,* October 1999, 30.

20. Randall Walker, Clark County director of aviation, interview by author, Las Vegas, December 22, 2000.

21. Courtwright, *Sky as Frontier,* 208. Also see Petzinger, *Hard Landing,* 426–427.

22. United States President William Jefferson Clinton's Remarks, White House Conference on Travel and Tourism, October 30, 1995, *Public Papers of the Presidents of the United States: William Jefferson Clinton, 1996* (1996), 1694. Also see Remarks on Signing Enabling Legislation for the National Commission to Ensure a Strong, Competitive Airline Industry, April 7, 1993, *Public Papers of the Presidents of the United States: William Jefferson Clinton, 1994* (1994), 412–414.

23. Rothman, *Neon Metropolis,* 253.

24. Ibid.

25. Busch interview.

26. *Delta Airlines Facts,* Delta Airlines, 1987, 2, http://www.delta.com/about_delta /index.jsp. Also see "Delta's Presence Here Adds $3 Million Annually," Delta Airlines Newsletter, July 1, 1981, Delta Airlines Collection, Atlanta.

27. Jennifer Michels, "Open Skies Agreement Bringing Global Dollars Home," *Airport Magazine,* February 12, 2001, 1–3, http://www.gsa.gov/portal/ext/public/site /FTR/file/Chapter301p010.html/category/21868/-124k–*Cached.*

28. *Las Vegas Sun,* June 11, 1998, E6.

29. Clark County Department of Aviation, "McCarran 2000: Reflections of the Past," 34.

30. Landrum and Brown Consultants, Master plan for McCarran Airport, II-2.

31. Bechtel Civil, Inc., McCarran International Airport Historical Report, 1981– 1987, 5–8. Landrum & Brown Consultants, Executive Summary, April 1976, VI-7, II-10.

32. Landrum and Brown, Executive Summary, April 1976, VI-7.

33. Clark County Department of Aviation, "Vision 2020: A Balanced Approach to Airport Development," 4.

34. *Las Vegas Review-Journal,* May 22, 1975, 17.

35. Ibid.

36. Michels, "Open Skies Agreement," 1.

37. Clinton's Remarks to the White House Conference on Travel and Tourism, October 30, 1995.

38. Bilateral Agreement with Japan on January 30, 1998, *Public Papers of the Presidents of the United States: William Jefferson Clinton, 1999* (1999), 146.

39. Bob Broadbent, Clark County director of aviation, interview by author, Las Vegas, July 14, 1998.

40. John Hanks, manager of international marketing, McCarran International Airport, telephone interview by author, January 19, 2008.

41. Las Vegas Convention and Visitors Authority, "London Calling: Las Vegas Welcomes Inaugural Flight of Gatwick-to-McCarran Connection Next Thursday, June 8" (press release), June 1, 2000. Also see Las Vegas Convention and Visitors Authority,

"Daily Nonstop Mexico–Las Vegas Flights to Begin Mid-June" (press release), May 16, 2000, http://www.lvcva.com.

42. Las Vegas Convention and Visitors Authority, "Daily Nonstop Mexico–Las Vegas Flights to Begin Mid-June."

43. Ibid.

44. Clark County Department of Aviation, "McCarran 2000: Reflections of the Past," 23.

45. *Las Vegas Sun,* June 11, 1998, E8.

46. Ibid.

47. TRA Consultants Executive Summary, October 1, 1979, 2. Also see McCarran International Airport in Clark County Department of Aviation, "Jet Blast," December 1989, 2.

48. *Las Vegas Sun,* June 11, 1998, E4.

49. Ibid., 13E.

50. Clark County Department of Aviation, "McCarran 2000: Reflections of the Past," 47.

51. Ibid., 51.

52. Randall Walker, Clark County director of aviation, to the chairman of the House Transportation and Infrastructure Subcommittee on Aviation, October 5, 2000. Included in the letter was a study done by the FAA determining how costly delays at McCarran will impact the commercial airlines, FDCH Congressional Testimony, 10/05/2000, AN:32Y29990200005915.

53. Ibid.

54. Las Vegas Convention and Visitors Authority, "Fourth Quarter Summary," *Las Vegas Marketing Bulletin* 27 (Winter 2000): 1.

55. Busch interview.

56. Las Vegas Convention and Visitors Authority, *Las Vegas Marketing Bulletin* 27 (Winter 2000): 19.

57. Ibid. Also see *Las Vegas Review-Journal,* August 3, 1995, 1, 2.

58. National Airlines, "In Business Las Vegas Special Report," *Las Vegas Review-Journal,* August 10, 2001, A5, A6. Also see "Las Vegas Business," *Las Vegas Review-Journal,* June 30, 2000, 1; and Clark County Department of Aviation, "Vision 2020," 27.

59. Clark County Department of Aviation, "Vision 2020," 12, 16.

60. Ibid., 27, 30. Also see Walker interview, April 15, 2001.

61. National Airlines, "In Business Las Vegas Special Report," A2.

62. Clark County Department of Aviation, "Vision 2020," 7.

63. Land and Land, *A Short History of Las Vegas,* 156, 173.

64. Moehring and Green, *Las Vegas,* 210.

65. Land and Land, *A Short History of Las Vegas,* 209.

66. Las Vegas Convention and Visitors Authority, Integrated Marketing Plan for 2000–2001, 84.

67. Ibid.

68. Wanda Chan, director of hotel operations, Rio Resort and Casino Hotel, interview by author, Las Vegas, December 1, 2000.

69. Ibid.

70. Walker interview, April 15, 2001.

71. Clark County Department of Aviation, "McCarran 2000: Reflections of the Past," 27.

72. Moehring and Green, *Las Vegas,* 205.

73. W. R. Mahaffey, Delta Airlines district marketing manager, "Delta Celebrates 25 Years at Las Vegas" (letter to Delta Las Vegas employees), July 1, 1986, in Delta Airlines Collection.

74. Rothman, *Neon Metropolis,* 252.

75. Heppenheimer, *Turbulent Skies,* 274–275. Also see *Las Vegas Sun,* March 9, 2005, 1; and Petzinger, *Hard Landing,* 404.

76. *Public Papers of the Presidents of the United States: George H. W. Bush* (1991), 1611.

77. Remarks on Signing the Federal Aviation Administration Reauthorization Act, October 9, 1996, *Public Papers of the Presidents of the United States, William Jefferson Clinton 1997* (1998), 1793–1794.

78. Courtwright, *Sky as Frontier,* 219.

79. *Las Vegas Sun,* September 17, 2001, A6.

80. *Las Vegas Sun,* September 19, 2001, C1, C4.

81. *Las Vegas Review-Journal,* April 13, 2002, D3. Also see *San Francisco Chronicle,* September 15, 2002, E1.

82. *Santa Rosa (California) Press Democrat,* September 15, 2002, E1.

83. *Las Vegas Review-Journal,* September 29, 2001, B7.

84. Ibid., May 5, 1997, 1.

85. *Las Vegas Business Press,* November 5, 2001, 1.

86. Ibid.

87. *Las Vegas Review-Journal,* September 29, 2001, B7.

88. Tony Cook, "Week in Review: Clark County," *Las Vegas Sun,* December 24, 2007, 3.

89. David Strow, "Recovery Under Way: Businesses Beginning to Bounce Back from Hard Times," *Las Vegas Sun,* October 12, 2001, 1.

90. Ibid.

CHAPTER FIVE ▶ *Still Growing During Tough Times*

1. Las Vegas Convention and Visitors Authority, Passenger and Visitor Volume Online, http://www.lvcva.com/index.jsp.

2. Ibid.

3. *Las Vegas Review-Journal,* March 21, 2002, D1.

4. Ibid., September 15, 2001, B1.

5. *Las Vegas Sun,* January 8, 2003, C2. Also see *Las Vegas Review-Journal,* April 25, 2002, D2.

6. *Las Vegas Review-Journal,* March 22, 2008, D2.

7. *Wall Street Journal,* March 29, 2004, C3. Also see *New York Times,* April 24, 2003, C6, and April 26, 2003, B3.

8. *Las Vegas Review-Journal,* May 4, 2002, A1. Also see *Press Democrat,* September 15, 2002, E1.

9. Public Law 107-42, September 22, 2001, 229. Also see *Las Vegas Review-Journal,* January 1, 2002, D2.

10. *Spokesman (Spokane, Wash.) Review,* August 28, 2008, 1.

11. McLaughlin, *St. Louis Post-Dispatch.*

12. Ibid.

13. *Executive Travel Magazine,* May 3, 2008, 1.

14. *Las Vegas Review-Journal,* March 12, 2002, D1.

15. *Las Vegas Sun Online,* January 25, 2001, 1.

16. *Las Vegas Review-Journal,* March 16, 2002, D3.

17. *USA Today,* July 30, 2002, B1, B5.

18. Ibid.

19. McCarran International Airport Web site, http://www.mccarran.com.

20. *Las Vegas Review-Journal,* July 24, 2008, C1.

21. *Las Vegas Sun Online,* July 27, 2005, 1.

22. Ibid.

23. *Las Vegas Review-Journal,* March 16, 2002, D7.

24. McCarran International Airport Web site, http://www.mccarran.com.

25. *USA Today,* August 19, 2008, B3. Also see *Las Vegas Review-Journal,* August 27, 2008, A1.

26. *Las Vegas Review-Journal,* September 5, 2008, A1.

27. *USA Today,* May 1, 2008, A1.

28. Richard N. Velotta, "Vegas Officials Courted British Airways for a Decade," *Las Vegas Sun Online,* May 18, 2009, 3.

29. McCarran International Airport Web site, http://www.mccarran.com.

30. *Las Vegas Review-Journal,* September 29, 2001, D1. Also see *Las Vegas Sun,* September 20, 2001, C3.

31. *Las Vegas Review-Journal,* August 20, 2008, D1.

32. McCarran International Airport Web site, http://www.mccarran.com.

33. *Las Vegas Sun,* August 19, 2001, D1.

34. Ibid. Also see Clark County Department of Aviation, "Vision 2020," 15.

35. Clark County Department of Aviation, "Vision 2020," 15.

36. Richard N. Velotta, "Airport Officials Hope Rivals Will Pick Up US Airways' Flight Cuts," *Las Vegas Sun Online,* November 6, 2009, 1. Also see *Las Vegas Sun in Business,* November 6, 2009, 1–3.

37. Velotta, "Airport Officials."

38. *Las Vegas Sun Online,* December 24, 2007, 3.

39. *Las Vegas Sun,* December 16, 2003, 3. Also see *Las Vegas Review-Journal,* April 11, 1976, 4, and March 21, 2002, D2.

40. *Las Vegas Review-Journal* and *Las Vegas Sun,* May 2, 2002, 11.

41. *Las Vegas Review-Journal,* May 16, 2007, D1.

42. Ibid.

43. *Las Vegas Sun,* January 8, 2008, AA1. Also see Las Vegas McCarran International Airport News Release, "Terminal 3 More than 50% Complete," January 12, 2010.

44. *Las Vegas Review-Journal,* April 26, 2007, A6.

45. Ibid.

46. Jeff Simpson, "How the Airline Industry's Recent Financial Problems Affect Las Vegas," *Las Vegas Sun Online*, April 27, 2008, 8.

47. Ibid.

48. Jeff Simpson, "Wynn, Who Has an Early Winner, Plans an Encore," *Las Vegas Sun Online*, December 6, 2005, 2.

49. Jon Ralston, "Wynn's Las Vegas," *Las Vegas Sun*, February 18, 2005, 2.

50. Encore Online, http://www.wynnlasvegas.com/.

51. *Las Vegas Review-Journal*, September 21, 2007, A2.

52. Gary Thompson, "Adelson Blasts LVCVA, Competitors, Union," *Las Vegas Sun Online*, March 25, 1998, 3.

53. McCarran International Airport Web site, http://www.mccarran.com.

54. "Palazzo Venetian News and Views," *Las Vegas Sun Online*, August 26, 2008, 2–3.

55. *Las Vegas Sun Online*, October 23, 2008, 2.

56. *Las Vegas Review-Journal*, April 13, 2002, D8.

57. Rich Velotta, *Las Vegas Sun Online*, January 5, 2009, 1.

58. *Las Vegas Sun Online*, December 9, 2009, 1–2. Also see *Philadelphia Daily Inquirer*, July 13, 2008, B3.

59. David McGrath Schwartz, "Not Much to Celebrate This Nevada Day," *Las Vegas Sun Online*, October 30, 2009, 3. Also see J. Patrick Coolican, "Lessons Las Vegas Can Learn from the Rust Belt," *Las Vegas Sun Online*, October 11, 2009, 2.

60. U.S. Bureau of Labor Statistics Web site, 2009.

61. "Nevada Is Worse Off: Diversification Efforts Need to Be Redoubled in Great Recession," editorial, *Las Vegas Sun Online*, July 2, 2010, 1.

62. Liz Benston, "Harrah's Seeks More Guests from Abroad," *Las Vegas Sun Online*, September 7, 2009, 1–2.

63. Amanda Finnegan, "Wynn: Stimulus Plan Won't Solve City's Woes," *Las Vegas Sun Online*, April 10, 2009, 1–2.

64. Steve Kanigher, "Yet Another List We're Last on Pace of Economic Recovery," *Las Vegas Sun Online*, June 16, 2010, 1.

65. Ibid., 2.

66. Ibid.

67. Kathleen Hennessey, "Slump Means Identity Crisis for Las Vegas," *Las Vegas Sun Online*, January 1, 2009, 5.

68. Benston, "Harrah's Seeks More Guests from Abroad," 2.

69. Ibid., 1.

70. Ibid.

71. Mark Broadbent, "Transatlantic Open Skies Agreement," *Airport News Online*, March 31, 2008. Statistical data are also from the CRS Report for Congress, April 13, 2007, by Raymond Ahearn, Kristin Archick, and Paul Belkin of Foreign Affairs, Defense, and Trade Division, U.S. State Department Web site, http://www.aviation-news.co.uk/view_issue.asp. Also see the Federal Travel Regulation 301-10.136–301-10.

72. Broadbent, "Transatlantic Open Skies Agreement."

73. Michels, "Open Skies Agreement, 1.

74. McCarran International Airport news release, "McCarran International Airport & the LVCVA Welcome New Air Service from Paris," May 26, 2010, http://www.mccarran.com.

75. Ibid.

76. *Las Vegas Sun Online,* May 2, 2008, 1.

77. Ibid., May 15, 2008, 1.

78. City of Las Vegas Web site.

79. Michael Mishak, "Rory Reid Emphasizes Need to Remix Economy," *Las Vegas Sun Online,* October 15, 2009, 1–3.

80. Coolican, "Lessons Las Vegas Can Learn from the Rust Belt," 5.

81. World-Class Jewelry Center brochure, August 26, 2008.

82. Smith Centre for the Performing Arts Brochure, August 26, 2008.

83. Clive Irving, "Behind the New Mega-Airlines: What a United-Continental Merger Would Mean," *Condé Nast Traveler,* April 30, 2010, 2.

84. Ibid.

85. Boeing Company 787 "Dreamliner" Web site.

► *Conclusion*

1. Richard N. Velotta, "British Airways Begins Non-Stop Flights from London to Las Vegas," *Las Vegas Sun Online,* October 25, 2009, 1.

2. Ibid.

3. Richard N. Velotta, "British Airways to Start Daily Service to Las Vegas," *Las Vegas Sun Online,* May 17, 2009, 2. Also see Richard N. Velotta, "Vegas Officials Courted British Airways for a Decade," *Las Vegas Sun Online,* May 18, 2009, 3.

4. Richard N. Velotta, "British Airways Brings Plenty of Upside to Las Vegas," *Las Vegas Sun Online,* October 30, 2009, 2.

5. Velotta, "Vegas Officials Courted British Airways for a Decade," 1.

6. Ibid.

7. Ibid.

►

Bibliography

► *Primary Sources*

INTERVIEWS

Broadbent, Bob. Director of aviation, Clark County. Interview by Daniel Bubb. Las Vegas. July 14, 1998.

Busch, Duane. TWA executive station manager, Las Vegas. Interview by Daniel Bubb. Las Vegas. January 7, 2001.

Chan, Wanda. Director of hotel operations, Rio Resort and Casino Hotel. Interview by Daniel Bubb. Las Vegas. December 1, 2000.

Davis, Susan. Las Vegas marketing representative, Southwest Airlines. Interview by Daniel Bubb. Las Vegas. January 4, 2001.

Hanks, John. Manager of international marketing, McCarran International Airport. Telephone interview by Daniel Bubb. January 19, 2008.

Michael, Boyd. Chief pilot and director of pilot training, Hacienda Airlines. Telephone interview by Daniel Bubb. May 1, 2000.

Moore, William J. Interview by Elizabeth Harrington. Reno. 1981.

Myers, Jennifer. Marketing manager, America West Airlines. Telephone interview by Daniel Bubb. January 4, 2001.

Taylor, Richard. General manager, Hacienda Hotel. Interview by Daniel Bubb. Las Vegas. April 26, 2000.

Walker, Randall. Director of aviation, Clark County. Interviews by Daniel Bubb. Las Vegas. December 22, 2000, and April 15, 2001.

COLLECTIONS

Bible, Senator Alan, Collection. University of Nevada, Reno. Letters, memoranda, legal documents.

Brown, Walter Folger, Papers. Ohio Historical Society, Columbus. Letters, memoranda, legal documents.

Cannon, Senator Howard, Collection. Lied Library Special Collections, University of Nevada, Las Vegas. Letters, memoranda, legal documents.

Gragson, Las Vegas Mayor Oran, Archive. Lied Library Special Collections, University of Nevada, Las Vegas.

Lied Library Special Collections. University of Nevada, Las Vegas. Airline advertisements.

McCarran, Senator Patrick, Collection. Nevada Historical Society, Reno. Letters, memoranda, speech transcripts.

Western Airlines Collection. Delta Airlines Archive, Atlanta. Letters, pamphlets, press releases.

GOVERNMENT RECORDS

Clark County City Council. Minutes.

Clark County Commission. Minutes.

Las Vegas Census Records.

Las Vegas Chamber of Commerce. Minutes.

Office of the Federal Register. *Public Papers of the United States Presidents.* Washington, D.C.: National Archives Records Publishing, 1961–1999.

Public Law 107-42, 22 September 2001.

U.S. House Subcommittee on Aviation. House Committee on Transportation and Infrastructure. 106th Congress, October 1999. Transcripts of testimony by airline CEOs.

U.S. Office of the Federal Register. National Archives and Records Service. *Public Papers of the Presidents of the United States.* Washington, D.C.: National Archives Records Publishing, 1961–1999.

U.S. Senate Committee on Commerce. 106th Congress, July 2000. Transcripts of testimony by airline CEOs.

AIRPORT PLANS

Bechtel Civil, Inc. Master plan for McCarran Airport. State and Local Government Documents, Lied Library, University of Nevada, Las Vegas.

———. McCarran International Airport Historical Report, 1981–1987. State and Local Government Documents, Lied Library, University of Nevada, Las Vegas.

Landrum and Brown Consultants. Executive Summary. April 1976. State and Local Government Documents, Lied Library, University of Nevada, Las Vegas.

———. Master plan for McCarran Airport. State and Local Government Documents, Lied Library, University of Nevada Las Vegas.

Leigh Fisher and Associates. Master plan for McCarran Airport. State and Local Government Documents, Lied Library, University of Nevada, Las Vegas.

TRA Consultants Executive Summary, October 1, 1979. State and Local Government Documents, Lied Library, University of Nevada, Las Vegas.

McCARRAN AIRPORT SUMMARIES

Clark County Commission. Dedication Program. McCarran Field, Las Vegas, December 19, 1948.

Clark County Department of Aviation. "McCarran 2000: Reflections of the Past." Clark County Commission airport summary. 2000.

———. "Vision 2020: A Balanced Approach to Airport Development." Clark County Commission master plan for McCarran Airport.

Las Vegas Convention and Visitors Authority. *Integrated Marketing Plan for 2000–2001.*
———. *Las Vegas Marketing Bulletin.* 1999, 2000, 2001.
———. Passenger and Visitor Volume Online. http://www.lvcva.com/index.jsp.

NEWSPAPERS

Arizona Daily Star
Arizona Republican
Boulder City Journal
Clark County Review
Las Vegas Business Press
Las Vegas Life
Las Vegas Review-Journal
Las Vegas Sun
Los Angeles Herald
Los Angeles Herald Examiner
Philadelphia Daily Inquirer
St. Louis Post-Dispatch
Salt Lake Tribune
San Francisco Chronicle
Santa Rosa (Calif.) Press Democrat
Southern California Rapid Transportation District Newsletter
Spokesman (Spokane, Wash.) Review
USA Today
Wall Street Journal
Washington Daily News
Washington Herald

► *Secondary Sources*

BOOKS

Armstrong, Ellis L., Michael C. Robinson, and Suellen M. Hoy, eds. *History of Public Works in the United States.* Washington, D.C.: American Public Works Association, 1976.
Bender, Marylin, and Selig Altschul. *The Chosen Instrument: Pan Am, Juan Trippe, the Rise and Fall of an American Entrepreneur.* New York: Simon and Schuster, 1982.
Biddle, Wayne. *Barons of the Sky.* New York: Simon and Schuster, 1991.
Biederman, Paul. *The United States Airline Industry: End of an Era.* Westport, Conn.: Praeger, 1982.
Bilstein, Roger E. *The Enterprise of Flight: The American Aviation and Aerospace Industry.* Washington, D.C.: Smithsonian Institution Press, 2001.
———. *Flight in America: From the Wrights to the Astronauts.* Baltimore: Johns Hopkins University Press, 1984.
———. *Flight Patterns: Trends of Aeronautical Development in the United States, 1918–1929.* Athens: University of Georgia Press, 1983.

Bowdoin, Van Riper. *Imagining Flight: Aviation and Popular Culture.* College Station: Texas A&M University Press, 2004.

Boyne, Walter J. *The Influence of Air Power upon History.* Gretna, La.: Pelican, 2003.

Boyne, Walter J., and Donald S. Lopez. *The Jet Age: Forty Years of Jet Aviation.* Washington, D.C.: Smithsonian Institution Press, 1979.

Brooks, Peter W. *The Modern Airliner: Its Origin and Development.* New York: Putnam, 1961.

Carpenter, Paul. *Phoenix Sky Harbor International Airport: The First 50 Years, 1935–1985.* Phoenix: Phoenix Aviation Department, 1985.

Caughey, John. *The American West: Frontier and Region.* Los Angeles: Ward Ritchie Press, 1969.

Corbett, David. *Politics and the Airlines.* London: Allen and Unwin, 1965.

Corn, Joseph. *The Winged Gospel: America's Romance with Aviation, 1900–1950.* New York: Oxford University Press, 1983.

Courtwright, David T. *Sky as Frontier: Adventure, Aviation, and Empire.* College Station: Texas A&M University Press, 2005.

Crouch, Thomas D. *Wings: A History of Aviation from Kites to the Space Age.* New York: W. W. Norton, 2003.

Daly-Bednarek, Janet. *America's Airports: Airfield Development, 1918–1947.* College Station: Texas A&M University Press, 2001.

Davies, R. E. G. *Airlines of the United States Since 1914.* London: Putnam, 1972.

——. *Rebels and Reformers of the Airways.* Washington, D.C.: Smithsonian Institution Press, 1987.

Denton, Sally, and Roger Morris. *The Money and the Power: The Making of Las Vegas and Its Hold on America, 1947–2000.* New York: Alfred A. Knopf, 2001.

Edwards, Elbert B. *200 Years of Nevada: A Story of People Who Opened, Explored, and Developed the Land.* Salt Lake City: Publishers Press, 1978.

Edwards, Jerome. *Pat McCarran: Political Boss of Nevada.* Reno: University of Nevada Press, 1982.

Elliott, Gary E. *The New Western Frontier: An Illustrated History of Greater Las Vegas.* Carlsbad, Calif.: Heritage Media, 1999.

Elliott, Russell R. *History of Nevada.* Lincoln: University of Nebraska Press, 1973.

Findlay, John M. *Magic Lands: Western Cityscapes and American Culture After 1940.* Berkeley and Los Angeles: University of California Press, 1992.

——. *People of Chance: Gambling in American Society from Jamestown to Las Vegas.* New York: Oxford University Press, 1986.

Frederick, John H. *Commercial Air Transportation.* Homewood, Ill.: Richard D. Irwin, 1961.

Grossman, Peter Z. *American Express: The Unofficial History of the People Who Built the Great Financial Empire.* New York: Crown, 1987.

Hawley, Ellis W. *The New Deal and the Problem of Monopoly: A Study in Economic Ambivalence.* New York: Fordham University Press, 1995

Heppenheimer, T. A. *Turbulent Skies: The History of Commercial Aviation.* New York: John Wiley, 1995.

Hudson, Kenneth. *Air Travel: A Social History.* Totowa, N.J.: Rowman and Littlefield, 1972.

Hulse, James N. *The Silver State: Nevada's Heritage Reinterpreted.* Reno: University of Nevada Press, 1998.

Jones, Michael D. *Desert Wings: A History of Phoenix Sky Harbor International Airport.* Tempe: Jetblast Publications, 1997.

Kennedy, Paul M. *The Rise and Fall of the Great Powers: Economic Change and Military Conflict from 1500 to 2000.* New York: Random House, 1988.

Komons, Nick A. *Bonfires to Beacons: Federal Civil Aviation Policy Under the Air Commerce Act, 1926–1938.* Washington, D.C.: U.S. Department of Transportation, Federal Aviation Administration, 1978.

Kropp, Phoebe. *California "Vieja": Culture and Memory in a Modern American Place.* Berkeley and Los Angeles: University of California Press, 2006.

Land, Barbara, and Myrick Land. *A Short History of Las Vegas.* Reno: University of Nevada Press, 1999.

Leary, William M. *Aerial Pioneers: The United States Air Mail Service, 1918–1927.* Washington, D.C.: Smithsonian Institution Press, 1985.

——. *Aviation's Golden Age: Portraits from the 1920s and 1930s.* Iowa City: University of Iowa Press, 1989.

Linn, Edward. *Big Julie of Las Vegas.* New York: Walker Press, 1974.

McCracken, Robert D. *Las Vegas: The Great American Playground.* Reno: University of Nevada Press, 1996.

Moehring, Eugene P. *Resort City in the Sunbelt: Las Vegas, 1930–2000.* Reno: University of Nevada Press, 1989.

Moehring, Eugene P., and Michael S. Green. *Las Vegas: A Centennial History.* Reno: University of Nevada Press, 2005.

Nugent, Walter. *Into the West: The Story of Its People.* New York: Alfred A. Knopf, 1999.

Ogburn, William. *The Social Effects of Aviation.* Boston: Houghton Mifflin, 1946.

Petzinger, Thomas Jr. *Hard Landing: The Epic Contest for Power and Profits That Plunged the Airlines into Chaos.* New York: Three Rivers Press, 1996.

Pomeroy, Earl. *The American Far West in the 20th Century.* New Haven: Yale University Press, 2008.

Ragsdale, Kenneth B. *Austin, Cleared for Takeoff: Aviation, Businessmen, and Growth of an American City.* Austin: University of Texas Press, 2004.

Reid, Edward, and Omar Demaris. *The Green Felt Jungle.* New York: Trident Press, 1963.

Reinhold, Ruth M. *Sky Pioneering: Arizona in Aviation History.* Tucson: University of Arizona Press, 1982.

Roske, Ralph. *Las Vegas: A Desert Paradise.* Tulsa: Continental Heritage Press, 1986.

Rothman, Hal K. *Devil's Bargains: Tourism in the Twentieth-Century American West.* Lawrence: University Press of Kansas, 1998.

——. *Neon Metropolis: How Las Vegas Started the Twenty-First Century.* New York and London: Routledge, 2003.

Rothman, Hal, and Mike Davis, eds. *The Grit Beneath the Glitter: Tales from the Real Las Vegas.* Berkeley and Los Angeles: University of California Press, 2002.

Russo, Gus. *The Outfit: The Role of Chicago's Underworld in the Shaping of Modern America.* New York: Bloomsbury Press, 2001.

Rust, Daniel L. *Flying Across America: The Passenger Experience.* Norman: University of Oklahoma Press, 2009.

Sampson, Anthony. *Empires of the Sky: The Politics, Contests, and Cartels of the World's Airlines.* Philadelphia: Coronet Books, 1985.

Schwantes, Carlos A. *Going Places: Transportation Redefines the Twentieth-Century West.* Bloomington: Indiana University Press, 2003.

Sciullo, Henry A., and Lawrence Danduran. *The Economic Impact of McCarran International Airport.* Las Vegas: Marketing Research and Development, 1977.

Serling, Robert. *The Only Way to Fly: The Story of Western Airlines, America's Senior Air Carrier.* New York: Doubleday, 1976.

Sheehan, Jack, ed. *The Players: The Men Who Made Las Vegas.* Reno: University of Nevada Press, 1997.

Smith, Henry Ladd. *Airways: The History of Commercial Aviation in the United States.* New York: Alfred A. Knopf, 1942.

Solberg, Carl. *Conquest of the Skies: A History of Commercial Aviation in the United States.* Boston: Little, Brown, 1979.

Steffens, Jerome O. *The American West: New Perspectives, New Dimensions.* Norman: University of Oklahoma Press, 1982.

Torgerson, Dial. *Kerkorian: An American Success Story.* New York: Dial Press, 1974.

Van der Linden, Robert. *Airlines and the Air Mail: The Post Office and the Birth of the Commercial Aviation Industry.* Lexington: University Press of Kentucky, 2002.

Whitnah, Donald R. *Safer Skyways: Federal Control of Aviation, 1926–1966.* Ames: Iowa State University Press, 1966.

Wilbur, Ray Lyman, and Arthur Mastick Hyde. *The Hoover Policies.* New York: Charles Scribner and Sons, 1937.

Wilson, Joan Hoff, and Oscar Handlin. *Herbert Hoover: Forgotten Progressive.* Long Grove, Ill.: Waveland Press, 1992.

Wright, Frank. *Desert Airways: A Short History of Clark County Aviation, 1920–1948.* Las Vegas: Clark County Heritage Museum Press, 1993.

Wrobel, David M., and Patrick T. Long, eds. *Seeing and Being Seen: Tourism in the American West.* Lawrence: University Press of Kansas, 2001.

Wrobel, David M., and Michael C. Steiner, eds. *Many Wests: Place, Culture, and Regional Identity.* Lawrence: University Press of Kansas, 1997.

ARTICLES

Airways. October 1999.

Aviation Week and Space Technology. April 9, 1962.

Bubb, Daniel K. "Hacienda Airlines: A First-Class Airline for Coach-Class Passengers." *Nevada Historical Society Quarterly* 44 (Fall 2001): 238–249.

———. "McCarran International and Phoenix Sky Harbor International: Airport Expansion, Tourism, and Urbanization in the Modern Southwest." *Nevada Historical Society Quarterly* 45 (Winter 2002): 125–142.

———. "The Success and Failure of Presidential Policy on Commercial Air Travel." *Journal of Air Commerce* 71 (Fall 2006): 653–667.

———. "Transforming the Desert: Commercial Aviation as Agent of Change, Las Vegas, 1926–1945." *Nevada Historical Society Quarterly* 52 (Fall 2009): 198–212.

Burnham, Frank. "In the Crockett Tradition." *Flying,* October 1955, 20–28.

Churchill, Edward. "How to Build an Airport." *Western Flying,* April 1976, 36–38.

Davis, Lou. *Flying,* May 1961, 29.

Evensen, Jay D. "Vegas Air History Flies By." *Las Vegas Review-Journal* 4 (October 1985): 12.

Harrington, Elizabeth. "History of Aviation in Las Vegas Valley." *Nevadan,* August 22, 1976, 5.

Kaufman, Perry. "City Boosters, Las Vegas Style." *Journal of the West* (July 1974): 46–59.

Launius, Roger D. "Planes, Trains, and Automobiles: Choosing Transportation Modes in the Twentieth-Century American West." *Journal of the West* 42 (Spring 2003): 45–55.

Launius, Roger D., and Jessie L. Embry. "Fledgling Wings: Aviation Comes to the Southwest, 1910–1930." *New Mexico Historical Review* 70 (January 1995): 1–27.

Lukas, Paul. "On the Wings of Commerce." *Fortune,* March 22, 2004, 1–5.

Lyth, Peter J., and Marc L. Dierkix. "From Privilege to Popularity: The Growth of Leisure Air Travel Since 1945." *Journal of Transport History* 15 (September 1994): 97–116.

McLaughlin, Tim. *St. Louis Post-Dispatch,* September 19, 2005, A1, A2.

Michels, Jennifer. "Open Skies Agreement Bringing Global Dollars Home." *Airport Magazine,* February 12, 2001, 1–3. http://www.gsa.gov/portal/ext/public/site/FTR/file/Chapter301p010.html/category/21868–124k–*Cached.*

Newman, Andy. "When Everybody Dined First Class: Coast to Coast by Jet in 1959." *New York Times,* January 26, 2009, A18.

Palermo, Dave. "Kirk Kerkorian: The Reticent Billionaire." In *The Players: The Men Who Made Las Vegas,* edited by Jack E. Sheehan, 163. Reno: University of Nevada Press, 1997.

Parrish, Wayne W. "New Aviation Power Center: Las Vegas." *American Aviation* 3 (February 1969): 14–16.

Rothman, Hal. "Tourism as Colonial Economy: Power and Place in Western Tourism." In *Power and Place in the North American West,* edited by Richard White and John Findlay. Seattle: Center for the Study of the Pacific Northwest, 1999.

Rust, Daniel. "Flying Across America: The Airline Passenger Experience and the West." *Montana: The Magazine of Western History* (Fall 2007): 3–21.

Stamos, George Jr. *Las Vegas Review Magazine,* August 12, 1979.

Taylor, Richard. *Casino News,* July 27, 1990.

THESES AND DISSERTATIONS

Bubb, Daniel K. "Thunder in the Desert: Commercial Air Travel and Tourism in Las Vegas, 1959–2001." Master's thesis, University of Nevada, Las Vegas, 2001.

Karsner, Douglas G. "'Leaving on a Jet Plane': Commercial Aviation, Airports, and Post-Industrial American Society, 1933–1970." Ph.D. diss., Temple University, 1993.

Skidmore, Mark. "Gaming Junkets in Nevada." Master's thesis, University of Nevada, Las Vegas, 1990.

Walters, Larry Alan. "A Study of Gambling Junkets Within the US Gaming Industry." Master's thesis, Cornell University, 1979.

UNPUBLISHED ARTICLES

Embry, Jessie L. "Air Travel in the Southwest."

———. "Building the Infrastructure: The Federal Government and Airports in the American West, 1930s."

———. "Entertainment of Transportation? Aviation in the West, 1910–1930."

Tyndall, Roger. "United Airlines in Las Vegas." University of Nevada, Las Vegas.

Index